CHILENISMOS
A Dictionary and Phrasebook
for Chilean Spanish

CHILENISMOS-ENGLISH

ENGLISH-CHILENISMOS

HIPPOCRENE DICTIONARY & PHRASEBOOKS

Albanian
Arabic(Eastern Arabic)
Arabic (Modern Standard)
Armenian (Eastern)
Armenian (Western)
Australian
Azerbaijani
Basque
Bosnian
Breton
British
Cajun French
Chechen
Croatian
Czech
Danish
Dari *Romanized*
Esperanto
Estonian
Finnish
French
Georgian
German
Greek
Hebrew *Romanized*
Hindi
Hungarian
Igbo
Ilocano
Irish
Italian
Japanese *Romanized*
Korean
Lao *Romanized*

Latvian
Lithuanian
Malagasy
Maltese
Mongolian
Nepali *Romanized*
Norwegian
Pashto *Romanized*
Pilipino (Tagalog)
Polish
Portuguese (Brazilian)
Punjabi
Québécois
Romanian
Romansch
Russian
Serbian
Shona
Sicilian
Slovak
Slovene
Somali
Spanish (Latin American)
Swahili
Swedish
Tajik
Tamil *Romanized*
Thai *Romanized*
Turkish
Ukrainan
Urdu *Romanized*
Uzbek
Vietnamese

CHILENISMOS
A Dictionary and Phrasebook for Chilean Spanish

CHILENISMOS-ENGLISH

ENGLISH-CHILENISMOS

Daniel Joelson

Hippocrene Books, Inc.
New York

Contacting the Author:
As with any language or dialect, Chilenismos will continue to evolve, so new words will be added to the lexicon and outdated ones will disappear. The author welcomes any comments about Chilenismos, concerning their history or the terms in this book, or those that you feel should have been included. All comments can be emailed to the author at comments@tastingchile.com. Additionally, you can find out more about Chilenismos at the author's Web site, www.tastingchile.com. The author strives to promote a broad discussion about the development of Chile's language, cuisine and culture.

Copyright © 2005 Daniel Joelson.

All rights reserved.

ISBN 0-7818-1062-0

For more information, address:
 HIPPOCRENE BOOKS, INC.
 171 Madison Avenue
 New York, NY 10016

Cataloging-in-Publication Data available from the Library of Congress.

Printed in the United States of America.

This book is for Anny.

Eres mi amor de Lota y mucho más.

Acknowledgements

I put this book together following extensive travels and intensive everyday experiences in Chile over several years in which I lived there. This entailed reading local papers and magazines, watching local television, and listening to the radio. However, the bulk of the terms came through conversations I had with Chileans throughout their beautifully long and lean country. For that reason, this book would not have been possible without the wonderful jokes, tales, side remarks and gags told by scores of Chileans.

While an entire list of those to whom I am grateful is impossible, here is a partial "most valuable" list. First and foremost, I would like to thank my wife, Anny, for all of the phrases she provided and for helping me to hash out the definitions of terms. A deep thank you also goes to her brothers Antonio and Luchito; her sister Eriquita; her mother Erika; her father Luis, and their cousin José Neira. Your boundless assistance helped carry this project forward.

Additionally, I give deep thanks to Hippocrene Books, for bringing this interesting dialect to the fore. In particular, I would like to thank Rebecca Cole, the editor, for all of her work. I would also like to thank the copy editor, Luisa Menares, for bringing to bear her own knowledge of Chilenismos, as well as designers, Susan Ahlquist and Ronnie McBride.

There are several others that I would like to specifically name. I give a special thank you to my good friend Andrés Musso for all of his assistance in finding words and phrases that I had not yet lunged upon. No, it certainly didn't hurt that I had a *huaso* from Curacaví at my side. Additional kudos goes to another good friend, Patricio Mas, in particular for his help in putting up my Web site. Furthermore, I offer my deepest gratitude to all of my friends from Valparaíso, especially Gabriel Flores and Rubén Parra, a couple of *porteños* with a love for language. I also would like to thank historian Hugo Rodolfo Ramírez and professor Alfredo Matus for their commentary on the subject of Chilenismos.

This list can only come to an end after I give one more thank you: to the Chilean people for all of their time, patience, and warmth in sharing their wonderful dialect with me. After that there's not much more to say except . . . ¡C–H–I–L–E, VIVA CHILE!

Table of Contents

Preface

Chile is known by tourists, expatriates, and the country's neighbors as having a vast amount of self-created words and idioms and peculiar mannerisms, making the language almost indiscernible even to native Spanish-speakers. For example, it is not unusual for Chilean movies to arrive into other Hispanophone cultures bearing subtitles. The films, *El chacotero sentimental* ("The Sentimental Teaser") and *Taxi para tres* ("Taxi for Three"), are just a couple of examples.

I began to make a list of these Chilenismos—all of the words, expressions, and grammatical quirks unique to Chile—in order to make my own life in Chile comprehensible, since every single day I would scratch my head at something a Chilean said that I later discovered was not in a dictionary nor in a textbook. I also found that the easiest way to fit in, get laughs, and be understood was to whip around Chilenismos at parties and dinners, stores and cafés, or any old corner of town.

The list gradually expanded until my goal became to compose a dictionary and phrasebook that could make the gringo's experience in Chile a more meaningful one. In fact, I would go as far as to say that if you plan on spending time in Chile it is almost as important to learn Chilenismos as it is to learn Spanish, since Chileans often sprinkle a Chilenismo or two into every single phrase.

To inject a bit more spice and reality into this book—Chileans aren't bashful with their own concoctions of slurs, epithets, and innuendos—I included many of those dirty, foul, and downright rude things that Chileans say every day.

As I discovered more about Chileans' great passion for their own diction, I also wanted this dictionary and phrasebook to be a tool for them. And I hope that it helps transport the Chilean expatriate back to his home country, or at least to remind him of how rich and entertaining Chilenismos are. Furthermore, due to Chile's free-trade treaty with the U.S. that took effect in January 2004 and the growing interest in English in Chile, this English-Chilenismos dictionary and phrasebook may serve as an aid for some Chileans to more easily access the English tongue.

Introduction

The History of Chilenismos

When the Spanish invaders arrived in Chile in the mid 1500s, they struggled to understand the local language, the indigenous Mapuche tongue known as *Mapudungun*. Though they often stumbled when trying to speak the alien language, the Spaniards adapted some of the words that they heard. The Spaniards were not able to subjugate the Mapuche and extinguish their language overnight. For hundreds of years the Mapuche put up fierce resistance, helping earn them the reputation as an indigenous people that could not be suppressed. In fact, approximately 1 million Mapuche still live in Chile. While some remain fiercely independent, many have assimilated into the larger society. This protracted interaction between the Mapuche and the Spanish may help explain why Chileans seem to use more non-Spanish words than other Latino nations. Many people with Spanish studies under their belt arrive to Chile and ask: What are they saying anyway?

Of course, the language the Spaniards brought is known as *español* or *castellano* (Castilian Spanish) in English. However, what is now widely spoken in Chile is referred to as "Chilenismos." Rather than elevating this widespread diction to the status of "language," some refer to it as a dialect or merely as a massive collection of invented words. But whatever it's called, it is important that one tries to grasp it when arriving in Chile because all Chileans speak it. While Chilenismos may not derive from the Spanish and Mapuche languages alone, their influence is undeniable. For example, the Chilenismo words *huichicheo* (mockery) and *huichipirichi* (a childish shriek) have discernible Mapuche origins. Words beginning with *hu* are prevalent in the Mapuche dictionary, as they are in Chilenismos, though for the latter *hu* often becomes *gu*. The pronunciation for these words is the same.

The indigenous Quechua peoples, found in northern Chile, have also had a profound influence on Chilenismos. Some words have been outright adopted by Chileans, such as *yapa*, a Quechua word meaning little gift. Other words have been only slightly altered, such as the Chilenismo *palta*. This comes from the Quechua and Aymara term *phalta*, meaning avocado. Other Latin countries typically refer to avocado as *aguacate*.

Alfredo Matus, a linguistics professor at the University of Chile and Director of the Chilean Academy of Language in Santiago, notes that all languages have geographical variations, but this is particularly true when there is major territorial expansion, as was the case with the language of the Spaniards, which is spoken today in many countries and on different continents. With such great geographical distance separating Spanish-speakers worldwide, it is only natural that local words began to develop and remained somewhat confined, rather than incorporated into traditional Castilian Spanish.

Linguistic Ripples From Latin America

While Chile's dialect remains distinct, its neighbors have played major roles in shaping the country's national verbiage. For instance, the word *bacán* or *vacán* (awesome) is a slang word used in Argentina that Chilean youths readily embraced. The word was first used in *el lunfardo,* the language of Argentine criminals and lowlifes. (Lunfardo's own history is rich, as the language was originally used in the Argentine tango world.) Constantly looking for a new hideaway many troublemakers raced across borders, with Argentines sneaking into Chile and Chileans creeping into Argentina. The criminals who crossed paths shared stories, techniques, and yes, dialects too. The *lunfardo* tongue directly affected *coa*, the tongue of Chilean criminals (see page 5).

Most Chileans don't pick up words on the sly, though, with knives bulging from their pants and a cohort on the corner shouting the newest codes. The couch-potato route is equally effective and certainly more common. Chileans often pick up expressions from television shows of other Latin countries that are beamed into their homes, such as the popular Mexican sitcom, *El Chavo del Ocho*. Still memorable today is the decades-old, oft-cited television commercial for a type of pasta, in which a mother cried to her Italian son: *"A mangiare, Tonino!"* That is: "Come and eat, Tonino!" Now, Chileans often say *"¡A manyar!"* for "Let's eat!" Derogatory and filthy words also filtered into Chile from abroad: The frequently-open hostility towards the gay community in Cuba gave rise on the island to the word *fleto* for homosexual, which Chileans now regularly use.

Venezuelans and Chileans share terms such as *sapo*, which refers to someone who keeps their ears to the ground and then spills the beans. Furthermore, Venezuelans refer to 1,000 bolivares (the Venezuelan currency) as a *luca*, just as Chileans do to 1,000 Chilean pesos. Venezuelans and Chileans also cooked up the word *luquear*. However, the two have ascribed different meanings to the words which sheds a bit of light on how words originate differently. For example, Venezuelans use the reflexive verb, *luquearse*, to mean "to make a lot of money"—as in a lot of *lucas*—from a thriving business. In contrast, for Chileans *luquear* means to look and its first syllable is pronounced similar to the English word, attesting to the word's anglo origins.

While the roots of some Chilenismos are less than noble, like that of *coa*, others come from the most revered of traditions. For there is a Latin influence on Chilenismos as well. This is owed to the persistently fierce influence from the Catholic Church, where Latin was imperative in past centuries, according to Hugo Rodolfo Ramírez, historian at Catholic University in Santiago. From the arrival of the conquistadores in Chile until the beginning of the twentieth century, parochial schools obligated students to study Latin and Greek, and many of the words they invented were derived from these studies.

Class Factors

Some Chilenismos arose as a result of class issues, with poor people (known as *los flaite*) referring to wealthier people (sometimes called *cuicos*) in no uncertain terms, and vice versa. This has a historical basis as well. Some of the Spanish conquistadores settled in Chile and became the aristocratic land-owning class. These well-educated and sophisticated people looked down on the lower-class and referred to them as *rotos*, or "broken ones." Today in Chile, in the midst of a heated argument, you might hear one person vituperate the other as being *roto*, which today means "someone vulgar or without grace."

Coa

Many of the popular words that Chileans use today, though, do have humble and racy origins. The dialect of *coa* frequently seeps into Chilean speech, constituting a notable source of Chilenismos. *Coa* originally developed in jails where inmates used it as a code so that guards could not understand what they were saying. Delinquents on the street also used specially invented words so that police and others could not understand them. Today, people in the subculture known commonly as *los flaite* use *coa* regularly, as do prisoners.

Many Chileans unrelated to this subculture also use many *coa* words. Yet, to complicate matters, since *los flaite* and prisoners still use code words, they are constantly adding new words to this dialect in order to keep the authorities off their tails. Just some of the *coa* words that have been adopted by the Chilean culture at large are: *a todo ritmo, echar la foca, una gamba, hacer perro muerto,* and *tiquitaca.*

Anglicismos

Words adopted by Argentina's *lunfardo* and Chile's *coa* often sound strangely English. Without a doubt, Chile is in many ways an anglophile nation. The

British played an important role in Chile in past centuries, particularly the nineteenth century, swarming to cities like Valparaíso for commercial reasons. Some British customs stayed with Chileans, such as the habit of taking a late afternoon tea.

Likewise, Chileans gradually incorporated many English words into their daily parlance. Just to provide a couple of examples, the Chilean term *bluyines* means blue jeans, and then there's the aforementioned Chilenismo *luquear*. The anglophile bent is owed in part to the United States, since Chileans are inundated with American music, movies, video games, and the like. Further, while French was once the most important second language for Chileans to learn—it was something the privileged class could flaunt—English now vastly supercedes French as a form of instruction in Chilean schools.

And English words aren't reserved for the classroom alone. While Chileans can be terribly creative with words, they also are sometimes called *copiones*, or copycats. They like to emulate the best practices from other cultures, and that includes borrowing words. Indeed, in linguistics the words that become part of everyday Chilean speech are referred to as *préstamos*, or loans. Such English words are referred to as *anglicismos* (anglicisms).

Some words, such as *bluyines*, are adapted from the English, while others remain *tal cual*, or "as is," in proper English. For example, words such as "performance" and "top" are used in Chile as if they were Chilean words, though they are spelled and pronounced as they are in anglophone cultures. This is hardly a linguistic aberration. Just as some anglophones use German words like *zeitgeist* or French words like *laissez-faire* because no English word has quite the same meaning, the English words that Chileans use often lack an ideal Spanish translation.

Phrases such as *a todo morrison* (or *a todo morri*) show how words come from English, are adopted by Chile's *coa* subculture, and ultimately end up as Chilenismos in the culture at large. This phrase, meaning "at full blast" or "no holes-barred," ostensibly comes from another Chilean expression, *a todo ritmo*, having the same meaning. Chileans inverted the syllables of the last word to get *morit*, and as is common in Chile, the last letter quickly vanished when spoken. Soon enough, *mori* became *morrison*, probably because it sounded better. Chileans enjoy drawing upon English words and names, and this term likely evolved from the widespread adoration of deceased singer Jim Morrison of The Doors.

In fact, while Chileans have fully adopted some English words, they have twisted others to suit their needs and sense of humor. For example, a red-head in Chile is called a *fanta*, in homage to the much-consumed orange soda bearing the same name. The English names Cindy and Wendy, are also used. In Chilenismos they become *cindy* and *güendy* and mean respectively, toothless and terrific. The former is a shortened version of *sin dientes*, which became *sin di*, and finally *cindy*. Another example that points to the more comical roots of some Chilenismos is the word menstruation, which in Spanish is either *el periodo* or *la regla*. *La regla* has another translation in English, "ruler," and Chileans have taken to simply referring to menstruation as *la ruler*.

In order to highlight those English words that have been adopted, this book contains a brief chapter of anglicismos, which follows the Chilenismo dictionary (see page 83).

Who Uses Chilenismos and When and Where?

Make no mistake about it: Castilian Spanish is the official language of Chile. And almost all Chileans speak Spanish, including many of the indigenous Mapuche. However, Chilenismos are not used by the few or only on special occasions. Rather, people of all classes, ages, and genders throughout the country use these words in daily conversation.

Chileans do not use Chilenismos at all times though. An analogy can be made with Ebonics, the dialect used among some African-Americans in the United States. The African-American community draws upon words from their self-created language (or dialect) with such frequency and passion that some have pressed for it to be accepted as a national tongue in the U.S. In practice, many African-Americans speak Ebonics at home or on the street, but when outside of their community (such as in white-dominated offices) they speak standard English.

In some ways, Chilenismos is similar. Many of these words also emerged "from the streets," gradually growing to form an entire vocabulary and dwarfing in importance the national language in certain communities or subcultures. Additionally, as with speakers of Ebonics, Chileans often change their locution according to circumstances, just as all of us (often unwittingly) do. So if a Chilean businessman has an important meeting with a group of executives that he is not familiar with, Chilenismos will be few-and-far between in the conversation. And in Chile, television newscasters and the top newspapers use a relatively small number of Chilenismos.

Yet, in comparison to Ebonics, Chilenismos are not circumscribed. As noted, it is not just a subculture that uses them, but rather all Chileans use and understand them. Newspapers are riddled with Chilenismos, as are the airwaves, television shows, billboards, schools, locker rooms, restaurants and bars, and everywhere else. It is seldom gauche to use them. On the contrary, they are de rigeur.

And while I recommend that you address the president of the Republic of Chile in Spanish, if you have the good fortune of meeting him or her, you can bet that the president would understand you very well if you tossed out a few Chilenismos for size. In fact, President Ricardo Lagos was asked to comment on a collective public nude photo in Santiago. His response: "*Esto habla de un país en buena onda.*" Roughly translated this means: "this shows that Chile is a cool country." *Buena onda* is a Chilenismo that means "cool," though its literal translation in Spanish is "good wave."

There is not always a simple explanation for the rise of certain Chilenismos and Chileans' unique speech patterns. But as Chileans often say in a quick turn of a phrase to characterize their own inscrutability: "*Es que así somos los chilenos.*" Or, "this is simply how we Chileans are."

Chilean Grammar and Speech

Basic Grammar Rules

- The *tú* Form

  Chileans incorporate standard Spanish grammar, except for the informal form of the second-person singular, "you." "You" is translated as *usted* in the formal form of Spanish. The informal way of saying "you" is typically *tú* in Spanish-speaking cultures. In some cultures, however, the informal *vos* is also used.

  Chile uses *tú*, but also changes the endings of proper Castilian Spanish. Words that typically end with an *s* sound in Spanish end with the sound of *ee* or a long *i*. *¿Te acordai?* ("Do you remember") instead of *¿Te acuerdas?* For –er and –ir verbs, the ending changes and is also accented for emphasis.

  Most often this "ai" is heard in the expression *¿Cachai?*, meaning "Do you understand?" On occasion, however, one does hear *¿Cachas?*, though *¿Cachas?* is still not Castilian because *cachar* is not a Spanish word that means to understand. Below is a comparison of standard Castilian and Chilenismo word endings in the *tú* form.

Standard Castilian	_Chilenismo_

–ar verbs (ex. mandar, to command)
| tú mandas | tú mand**ai** |

–er verbs (ex. comer, to eat)
| tú comes | tú com**í** |

–ir verbs (ex. pedir, to ask for)
| tú pides | tú ped**í** |

All verbs follow this rule, except for one odd exception. The Castilian _tú eres_, from the infinitive _ser_ (to be), is translated in Chilenismos to: _tú soy_. This borrows the standard Castilian first person singular ending (_yo soy_: I am) to make a second person singular construction. When non-Chileans hear _tú soy_, they scratch their head and translate it, "you I am," though it actually means "you are."

- Present vs. Future
  Chileans frequently use the present tense of a verb when they're talking about the near future. For instance, the Chilenismo expression, _Te presto ropa_, can mean "I will defend you," as opposed to "I defend you."

- Plurals
  Adding an _s_ to verbs in the past tense of the second person singular is also a unique Chilenismo construction. For example, "_¿Cómo dormistes?_" is the same as "_¿Cómo dormiste?_" This stylistic irregularity is in direct contrast to Chileans' predilection for dropping the _s_ on the end of nouns and adjectives.

Understanding Chilean Speech

• Chileans are extremely fond of using the diminutive endings, "*–ito*," and "*–ita*." Literally, this ending means "little" and is used in Spanish to refer to someone affectionately. So, for example, one could call Carlos "Carlitos" in order to show affection. However, in Chile the use of "*–ito*" and "*–ita*" are not merely done to call someone by their name in an affectionate way. Rather, almost every word can be—and is—made diminutive. Explanations for this vary, but a popular belief is that built into the Chilean psyche is an aversion to insulting or confronting others. Their desire to reach an agreement or accommodate others leads them to soften and sweeten words by converting them into the diminutive.

Consider the following sentence:
¿Querís pancito y cafecito para que estés calentita, Eriquita?

In typical Spanish this would be written: *¿Quieres pan y café para que estés cálida, Erika?* In English, this translates to: "Would you like some bread and coffee to warm you up, Erica?" [Note also that *calentita* becomes *cálida*, because in Chile *calentita* can mean nice and warm, but *caliente*, without the diminutive, means sexually aroused.] Most words made into the diminutive are nouns or adjectives, but that is hardly the rule, since there is even *Hasta lueguito* for "So long" or "See you later."

• In English almost all of us lapse into using ers and uhs, repeating the same word twice consecutively, or saying things that effectively mean nothing, such as "like" and "you know," to help us comfortably complete our phrases. Chileans are no different and rely on many such *muletillas*, which are little crutches. Among the phrases they turn to that don't fundamentally affect the meaning of a sentence include:

Digamos	Let's say
¿Cachai?	You understand? Ya know?
¿Me entendí?	You understand?
Es que	It's that
Ponte tú	For example (literally "Put yourself–you")
Fíjate, ¿Te fijas?	You understand/ You know (literally "Fix yourself")

- Chilenismos sometimes include apostrophes, while Castilian Spanish does not. In Chilenismos, apostrophes are used to indicate that a word is cut short. For instance, *para* becomes *pa'*, indicating that the final syllable is omitted.

- Often with nouns and adjectives that end in –ado, the *d* is dropped in pronunciation and the word's ending is pronounced differently. Chileans also often drop the *d* when spelling such words in an informal context. Thus, *pescado*, meaning fish, would be spelled *pescao*, and be pronounced "pess–cow," rather than "pess–ca–doe." The word *cansado*, meaning tired, would be pronounced "cahn–sow," rather than "cahn–sah–doe." Reducing words by one syllable and giving them more of a drawl is another form of shorthand. Because the *d* is often not dropped from "–ado" words, I have included it in spelling such words in the dictionary and phrasebook sections.

- As noted earlier, Chileans do not typically pronounce the *s* when it falls at the end of a word. Thus, *más o menos* sounds like "ma o meno." This is a major reason why Chilean Spanish is very difficult for the newcomer to understand. When confronted with this dilemma, you can ask Chileans to try to pronounce the *s* at the end of their words. The best practice, though, is to just try to get used to their *s* omissions.

- Chileans say certain things that you should not always take literally. For example, they often respond to another's comment by saying, "*perfecto.*" You should generally take this to mean, "Right," "OK," or "Good," rather than "That's perfect." This custom may come from the influence of the British, who are also known to declare less-than-stupendous things to be "brilliant" or "lovely."

- Chileans sometimes end words jokingly with the two-syllable ending of "–ation", as if they are speaking English. That is, many believe (and correctly so) that English is a language replete with words ending with "–ation" and so they play with that in their own language. For example, a Chilean might jokingly say, "*me duele la guateichon*" (instead of "*me duele la guata*"). Pronounced wah–tay–tion, it means, "My stomach hurts."

On Reading the Text

This dictionary and phrasebook is largely self-explanatory, but here are a few guidelines on how to better understand its structure and logic:

- One-word terms have been placed in the dictionary section while multiple-word terms are in the phrasebook. For example, *"chanta la moto"* ("slow down") is placed in the phrasebook, rather than in the dictionary. When they form part of a popular subject matter, some one-word terms are placed in a section of the phrasebook, as well as in the dictionary.

- Words that some Chileans believe to be Chilenismos, such as *lata* ("bore" or "shame"), are not included when they are found in most standard Spanish dictionaries. Such words are not Chilenismos.

- Some Chilenismos also have traditional Spanish definitions. That is, Chileans have invented new definitions for existing Spanish words. In those cases, I have included only the Chilenismo definition, but not the traditional Castilian definitions.

- As mentioned, Chileans did not invent all of the words in this book. Since there is great interchange among Latin American cultures, non-Castilian words used in Latin America sometimes cross borders and become fixtures. Those words that stuck in the Chilean culture are included in this book because they are not found in classic Castilian and because this book's purpose is to enable you to better understand Chileans, regardless of whether words or expressions herein can also be heard in other cultures. Linguists differ over whether words that did not originate in Chile can be considered Chilenismos. The majority view is that they indeed should be.

- As a soccer-crazed nation, Chile was bound to invent its own set of words for that sport (*fútbol*). Hispanophone soccer fans will not be surprised that *hacer el chileno* is not in this book. This term, meaning "to do a bicycle kick" (literally "to do the Chilean"), is used widely throughout Latin America.

Abbreviations

The list below indicates the abbreviations found in the text. As a guide, please note that when a noun is simply accompanied by an *n* it has both masculine and feminine forms. The masculine form of the word is provided in the text. The feminine noun is usually formed by replacing the *o* that ends the word with an *a*, or by adding an *a* if the word ends in a consonant. Some nouns have just one form, which is provided. For adjectives, the masculine form of adjectives is provided. The feminine form is also typically formed by dropping the last letter and adding an *a*.

adj.	adjective
adv.	adverb
derog.	derogatory
esp.	especially
idm.	idiom
indet.	indeterminate
infml.	informal
interj.	interjection
lit.	literary meaning
n.	noun
n.f.	feminine noun
n.m.	masculine noun
neg.pron.	negative pronoun
pl.	plural
prep.	preposition

pron.	pronoun
refl.	reflexive
sl.	slang
v.	verb

Chilenismos-English Dictionary

A

abutagado *adj.* choked, clogged
acartonado *adj.* rigid, inflexible
acato *adv.* here
achacado *adj.* sad, pained
achacar(se) *v.* to anger, sour on
achaplinarse *v.refl.* to repent, backtrack, become
    embarrassed
achoclonar *v.* to accumulate, pile up
achorarse *v.* to anger, get riled up
achunchado *adj.* timid, ashamed
achuntar *v.* to be right, be successful, be dead-on
agarrado *adj.* in love, attached
agarraguire *n.* glutton, hog (*infml. derog.*)
agarrar *v.* to touch, kiss
agilado *adj.* silly, stupid
agrandado *adj.* conceited, big for your britches
agringado *adj.* gringo-like (esp. in appearance,
    having Western features)
aguachar *v.* to pamper, take care of, pine for
aguaguado *adj.* infantile, spoiled
aguaitar *v.* to wait
aguja *adj.* importunate, annoying, insistent;
    quick-witted
agüeonado *adj.* silly, stupid
alaraco *adj.* exaggerated
alcahueta *adj.* refers to someone who protects
    another person's lies, someone who covers up
    someone else's wrongdoings

alegar *v.* to dispute, quarrel
aliñado *adj.* strong, tough, bold
alolado *n.* childish, youthful, immature
altirante *adv.* immediately, at once, in a moment
altiro *adv.* immediately, at once, in a moment
amachada *adj.* butch
amarrete *adj.* egoistic, stingy, greedy
amermelado *adj.* stupid, incompetent
amurrarse *v.refl.* to get angry, sulk
angurriento *adj.* hungry; greedy
aperarse *v.refl.* to supply, provide
aperrado *adj.* optimistic, resilient
apestado *adj.* fed up
apitutado *adj.* well-connected
apretado *adj.* stingy
arranado *adj.* ashamed, cowardly
arranarse *v.refl.* to become cowardly or ashamed
arrastrado *adj.* sycophantic, slavish
arratonarse *v.refl.* to become frightened; to repent
arrugón *n.* person who fails to fulfill promise
artesa *n.f.* hippy, artesan
artista *n.* personage (not necessarily an artist)
arturo *n.m.* 10,000 peso bill
aserruchar *v.* to rev up a car
asopado *adj.* foolish, dim-witted
asunteque *n.m.* matter, issue
atado *n.m.* problem, complication
atadoso *adj.* problematic, complicating
atinar *v.* to hook up (*sl.*), kiss; to wake up (to get a clue)
atorado *n./adj.* guarder of secrets
atracar *v.* to kiss
atraque *n.m.* kiss
attach *n.m.* attached file

B

bacán *adj.* awesome, cool, terrific
bachata *n.f.* house slipper

bajoneado *adj.* depressed, sad
bajonear *v.* to lower
barra; **barra brava** *n.f.* group of fans or
    hooligans
barsa *adj.* cheeky, presumptuous, shameless
beatle *n.m.* turtleneck
bebida *n.f.* soda, soft drink
benaiga *adj.* excellent, fantastic
benaiga *interj.* shucks
berma *n.f.* road shoulder
bicho *n.m.* spirit, insignificant person
bikingo *adj.* brutal
billullo *n.m.* money
bluyines *n.m.pl.* blue jeans
bocón *n.* blabbermouth
boliche *n.m.* small store
bolsear *v.* to mooch, sponge off of
bolsero *n./adj.* mooch, freeloader
bomba *n.f.* gas station; babe
botado (algo) *adj.* cheap, inexpensive; simple, easy
botado (alguien) *adj.* discarded, rejected; drunk
botella *adj.* solitary, lonely, unaccompanied
brígido *adj.* disagreeable, dense; dangerous
bronca *n.f.* anger, ire
bruja *n.f.* wife (nickname)
buche *adj.* selfish, hoggish
burra *adj.* silly, clumsy

C

caballo *adj.* terrific, cool, fantastic
cabreado *adj.* tired, bored, fed up
cabritas *n.f.pl.* popcorn
cabro *n.m.* boy, lad
cabra *n.f.* chick (*sl.*), gal
cabrón *n.* pimp, expert

cachaña *n.f.* ability, skill
cachar *v.* to understand, see
cacharpeado *adj.* well-dressed
cacharro *n.m.* old auto, clunker (*infml.*)
cachativa *n.f.* intuition, instinct
cachero *adj.* horny (*sl.*), sexually charged
cachete *n.m.* side of buttocks
cachetón *adj.* arrogant
cachilupi *adj.* cool, good, attractive, entertaining
cachinear *v.* to battle for a soccer ball
cachiporra *adj.* braggart
cachiporrearse *v.refl.* to boast
cachipún *n.m.* the hand game "rock, paper, scissors"
cachipurri *n.m.* sweetheart
cachito *n.m.* moment, second
cacho *n.m.* problem, dilemma
cachorra *n.f.* girl
cachorro *n.m.* boy
cachuchazo *n.m.* hit, blow
cachuo *n.m.* suspicious, doubtful
cachureo *n.m.* knick-knack, junk
cachurero *n.* someone who saves everything
cafiche *n.* exploiter, someone who uses another for
their money; pimp
cagado *adj.* chintzy, cheap; troubled, doomed
cagar (a alguien) *v.* to cheat on (one's mate)
cahuín *n.m.* lie, rumor
cahuinear *v.* to malign discreetly, stab in the
back (*idm.*)
cahuinero *n.* liar, rumormonger
calato *adj.* broke; nude
caldiao *adj.* hot
caldiarse *v.refl.* to get hot, heat up
caldúo *adj.* juicy
calentura *n.f.* sexual excitement
caleta *adv.* lots of, tons
califa *adj.* horny (*sl.*)

cálifont *n.m.* water heater

callampa *n.f.* diddly, nothing; shantytown; hat; bowl-shaped haircut

caluga *n.f.* stomach muscle; caramel

calugazo *n.m.* smooch, kiss

calzonero *n.m.* male soap opera fan; man dominated by his significant other

camarote *n.m.* bunk bed

cambucho *n.m.* handmade paper bag

camote *adj.* annoying, obnoxious

camotera *n.f.* playful slap

cana *n.f.* jail, can (*sl.*)

canchero *n.* stud (*sl.*); daring person, skillful person

canero *n.m.* longtime prisoner

canuto *adj.* protestant, zealous evangelist

canyengue *n.f.* party

caña *n.f.* hangover; small cup of wine

capaz *adv.* perhaps

caperuzo *adj.* clever, smart

capo *adj.* intelligent

caracha *n.f.* scab

caracho *n.m.* long face

carbonero *n.* rabble-rouser, agitator

cargado *adj.* full of money, loaded (*sl.*)

cargante *adj.* insistent

carnudo *adj.* attractive, handsome

carqueta *adj.* selfish, stingy

carrete *n.m.* party, night out, frolic

carretear *v.* to carouse, party

carretero *n.* reveler, party animal

cartucho *adj.* reserved, diffident; disingenuous

cascarrabias *adj.* stubborn, disobedient

casera *n.f.* miss

casero *n.m.* sir

casino *n.m.* cafeteria

castigarse *v.refl.* to reward oneself, spoil oneself

castizo *adj.* horny (*sl.*)

catear *v.* to look

cátedra *n.f.* test (school)

catete *adj.* insistent, stubborn

catetear *v.* to bug, bother

cebollento *adj.* vulgar, sleazy

cecilia *n.f.* thirst

chacal *adj.* cool, great

chacharear *v.* to converse, gossip

chachazo *n.m.* slap, whack

chachero *adj.* talkative, loquacious

chacoteo *n.m.* buffoonery, shenanigans

chacotero *n.* jovial person, joker, life of the party
     (*infml.*), card (*infml.*)

chacrearse *v.refl.* to worsen, depreciate, devalue,
     break down

chala *n.f.* sandal

chalupa *n.f.* house slipper

chambreado *adj.* warm (usually refers to
     heated wine)

champa *n.f.* bushy hair, big head of hair

chana *adj.* sleazy, vulgar

chancho *n.m.* burp

chanta *adj.* false, fake; mendacious

chantar *v.* to do, to execute (esp. with sports)

chao *interj.* finished, done

chape *adj.* doting

charcho *adj.* poor quality, bad

chatarra *n.f.* junk food, fast food

chato *n.m.* friend

chato *adj.* stuffed, sated; tired

chaucha *n.m.* money, dough (*sl.*)

chaucha *interj.* careful, watch out

chavela *interj.* good-bye

chela, chelita *n.f.* beer

chicha *n.f.* boozer; hard grape or apple cider

chicoca *n.f.* daughter

chicotear *v.* to hurry

chihua *adj.* low-life, vulgar

chimenea *n.f.* heavy smoker

chingana *n.f.* party, buffoonery; indigenous parties in Indian villages

chinita *n.f.* ladybug

chino *adj.* having Asian characteristics

chiporra *n.f.* girlfriend

chiporro *n.m.* pal, younger friend

chipotearse *v.refl.* to forget

chirola *n.m.* compliment

chispotear *v.* to break down, end

chiteco *n.m.* cloth

chiva *n.f.* lie, fabrication

chiviento *n.m.* liar

choca, choquita *n.f.* snack

chocho *n.m.* curl of hair

chocho *adj.* happy, content, proud

choco *n.m.* slab of wood; short person

choco *adj.* short

choreado *adj.* angry

chorear *v.* to steal

chori *adj.* entertaining, fun

choro *n.m.* change purse; mussel

choro *adj.* fearless, bold; depraved; excellent, terrific

chorrera *n.f.* multitude, great quantity

chotorrear *v.* to chat

chúcaro *n.* unmanageable, indomitable, rebel, fighter, warrior

chucheta *n.* rowdy person, crazy person

chuchunco *prep.* distant, far away

chueco *adj.* corrupt

chuliar *v.* to hang out with thugs

chulo *adj.* sleazy, slimy

chuncho *n.m.* owl; University of Chile soccer fan

chupalla *n.f.* hat

chupalla *interj.* darn, shucks

chupamedia *n.m.* sycophant, bootlicker, lapdog

chupilca *n.f.* hard cider with toasted flour
churreteado *adj.* dirty
churretear *v.* to dirty
chutear *v.* to kick; to jilt
cimarra *n.f.* hookey (*sl.*), truant
cinco *adj.* broke, neckless
cindy *adj.* toothless
citadino *n.m.* city person
cleta *n.f.* bicycle
clotear *v.* to break down, end
coa *n.f.* slang, street talk
cochino *adj.* filthy
cocido *adj.* drunk; burning up
cocoroco *adj.* flirtatious
cogote *n.m.* neck
cogotear *v.* to assault
cogotero *n.* assailant
cola *n.f.* rear-end
colaless *n.m.* thong
colegio *n.m.* elementary and junior high school
color *n.m.* exaggeration
coloriento *adj.* exaggerated
columpiar *v.* to mock, make fun of
comadre *n.f.* gal, friend
combinado *n.m.* Pisco brandy mixed with a soft
    drink (esp. Coke or Sprite)
combo *n.m.* slap, hit, punch
compadre *n.m.* pal, buddy
complicado *adj.* challenging
computín *n.* computer geek
comunacho *n.* communist
conchalevale *interj.* darn, shucks
concho *n.* youngest child; last drop, last item
condoro *n.m.* error, mistake
confort *n.m.* toilet paper
control *n.m.* quiz (in school)
coñete *adj.* greedy, stingy; overambitious

copete *n.m.* alcoholic drink
copeteado *adj.* drunk; hungover
copión *n.m.* copycat
copuchento *adj.* nosy, prying
cosita *n.f.* sweetheart, dear
cototo *n.m.* swelling
cototo *adj.* difficult; excellent
cuadros *n.m.pl.* underwear (women's)
cualquier *adj.* a lot, innumerable
cuático *adj.* exaggerated, larger-than-life,
    show-stealing
cucarro *n.* drunk
cuea *n.f.* luck
cueca *n.f.* Chile's national dance
cuernúo *adj.* deceived, cheated
cuestión *n.f.* thing, stuff
cueuo *adj.* lucky
cuico *n./adj.* yuppy, wealthy and arrogant person;
    wealthy
cuma *n./adj.* vulgar, coarse
cuneteado *adj.* awry, askew
curado *adj.* drunk
curarse *v.refl.* to get intoxicated
cursi *adj.* delicate

D

debilucho *adj.* weak
decaído *adj.* sick, tired, sad
defenderse *v.refl.* to get by, do all right,
    get along OK
demás *adv.* certainly; exceedingly so
denante *adv.* recently, a short while ago
denso *adj.* ill-humored, disagreeable
depre *n.f.* depression
desaforar *v.* to throw out of Congress

descartuchar *v.* to unbottle, liberate; to lose one's virginity

descuerar *v.* to malign

descueve *adv.* superbly, magnificently

desgarro *n.m.* phlegm

despelote *n.m.* disorder

destartalado *adj.* unkempt, messy

dije *adj.* polite, nice

doblada *n.f.* Chilean bread

doblado *adj.* drunk, drugged

ducha teléfono *n.f.* shower faucet (detachable)

dura *n.f.* truth

durazno *n.m.* peach

durazno *adj.* dim-witted; stubborn

E

educativo *n.m.* traffic ticket warning

embalado *adj.* smitten; rushed

embarado *adj.* silly

embarrar *v.* to ruin something, err

embrollar *v.* to trick

emilio *n.m.* email

empaquetado *adj.* formal-dressing, natty, dapper

empelotado *adj.* angry, livid

empelotarse *v.refl.* to anger, explode with fury; to disrobe

emperifollao *adj.* well-dressed, dapper

empilucharse *v.refl.* to disrobe

empinar *v.* to chug

emplumarse *v.refl.* to anger

emputecido *adj.* livid, furious

enajenado *adj.* angry

encachao *adj.* handsome, gorgeous

encalillado *adj.* indebted

encaramar *v.* to get on, go up

enchapado *n.m.* habit, custom
enchufarse *v.refl.* to rejoin a conversation after spacing out, regroup
encontrón *n.m.* dispute, fight
ene *adv.* a lot, very many
enganchado *adj.* smitten, in love
enganchar *v.* to pay attention, heed
engañito *n.m.* small gift
engrupir *v.* to lie, invent, sweet-talk
enojón *n.* someone easily angered, someone prickly, touchy
enrollado *adj.* involved, vexed
enrollarse *v.refl.* to obsess, involve oneself deeply
entonado *adj.* tipsy
entrar *v.* to enthuse (esp. used in negative)
envenado *adj.* angry
enyegüecer *v.* to become angry, go berserk (*sl.*); become aroused
enyegüesido *adj.* infatuated, temporarily smitten
escoba *adv.* likewise
espornocu *n.m.* zit, pimple
estampilla *adj.* doting
exquisito *adj.* finicky

F

facha *n.m.* sharp-dresser
facho *n.* right-winger
fanta *n.f.* red-head
farrear *v.* to goof around
feín *adj.* ugly
figurón *n.* attention-seeker
filete *n.* beauty
filo *interj.* no matter
flaco *n.* buddy, pal
flaite *n./adj.* vulgar, coarse

flato *n.m.* gas, burp
fleta *n.f.* slap, hit
fletar *v.* to hit, to kick out
fleto *n.m* queer, homosexual
flojear *v.* to laze, lounge
flopy *adj.* laid-back, relaxed
flor *adj.* beautiful
flor *adv.* fine, well
florerito *adj.* showy
flotador *n.* fatso
foca *n.m.* breath (esp. bad)
fofo *adj.* unathletic, lazy
fome *adj.* pathetic, lame, boring, tasteless
fomedad *n.f.* lameness, boredom
fomeque *adj.* pathetic, lame, boring
fomingo *n.m.* Sunday
fonda *n.f.* place of (independence) celebration
fondear *v.* to hide
fondo *n.m.* large cooking pot
forro *n.m.* dilemma
franchute *n./adj.* French person/French
fregado *adj.* strict, serious; difficult
fresco *adj.* bold, cheeky, sassy, exploitative
frigidaire *n.m* refrigerator
fritanga *n.f.* fried food
frito *adj.* screwed (*sl.*), doomed
frutilla *n.f.* strawberry
funa *n.f.* bad luck
funado *adj.* unmotivated, apathetic
funar *v.* to kill
funarse *v.refl.* to break down, end

G

gabriela *n.f.* 5,000-peso bill
galla *n.f.* gal

gallada *n.f.* pack, group, gang
gallito *n.m.* frog in throat (*idm.*), croak
gallo *n.m.* guy
gamba *n.f.* 100 pesos; big foot
gancho *n.m.* friend, buddy
gansa *n.f.* gal
ganso *adj.* foolish, stupid
ganso *n.m.* guy
gaña *n.f.* sand in the eyes from sleeping
garabato *n.m.* expletive
garetearse *v.refl.* to get lost
gargajo *n.m.* phlegm, spittle
gasuso *adj.* hungry, gluttonous
gauchada *n.f.* favor
gil *adj.* silly, stupid
gilberto *adj.* foolish, silly
girafa *n.* tall person
goma *n.m.* drudge, drone
gorrear *v.* to be unfaithful, cheat on
grandota *n.f.* large girl/woman
grandote *n.m.* large boy/man
Gringolandia *n.f.* the United States of America
gritón *n.* blabbermouth, yeller
groso *adj.* terrific, fantastic
grupiento *adj.* mendacious
grupo *n.m.* lie, deception
guachaca *adj.* low-class, vulgar, poor, coarse
guachipear *v.* to steal
guachito *n.* hunk, knockout
guacho *n.m.* orphan
guagua *n.f* baby; bus (small)
guagualón *n.* someone who acts like a baby
guajardo *n.m.* vomit
guanaco *n.m.* riot police vehicle
guarda *n.f.* warning
guarifaifa *n.f.* issue, thing, problem
guaripoleao *n.* drunk

guasca *n.f.* belt, strap
guascazo *n.m.* hit, whipping
guata *n.f.* belly, stomach
guata *adj.* (esp. women) overweight, ugly;
     vulgar, base
guater *n.m.* bathroom
guatero *n.m.* hot water bottle
guaton *n.m.* 1 million pesos
guatón *n./adj.* fat, fatso
güeá *n.f.* stupidity, crap
güehéta *adj.* idiotic
güendy *adj.* terrific, great
güeón *n./adj.* friend, buddy; punk, jerk, dolt (*derog.*)
guerrera *n.f.* pushover
güevada *n.f.* stupidity; thing
güevear *v.* to mock, kid
güeveo *n.m.* buffoonery, shenanigans, foolishness
güiña *n.* robber

H

hachazo *n.m.* hangover
hallulla *n.f.* type of bread
hawaiana *n.f.* flip-flop (i.e., shoes)
heavy *adj.* fantastic, cool (*sl.*)
high *adj.* rich
hinchar *v.* to bother
hocico *n.* big mouth
hocicón *n.* (person) blabbermouth
hongo *n.m.* nothing, diddly
huaso *n.* country person, bumpkin (*derog.*); stupid
     or naïve person (*derog.*)
huichicheo *n.m.* mockery
huichipirichi *interj.* Ha!, childish shriek
huifa *n.f.* thing, matter
huincha *n.f.* tape (adhesive)
huiro *n.m.* joint (marijuana); alga

I

igual *adv.* also; and; anyway
impeque *adj.* impeccable
impote *n.m.* lidded bowl
indio *n.* hot-tempered person, fiery
inflado *adj.* arrogant
inflar (a alguien) *v.* to heed, pay attention to
iñora *n.f.* wife

J

jaibón *n.* a noble, person of wealth
jajaja *interj.* ha-ha-ha
jalar *v.* to snort drugs
jalea *n.f.* Jell-O
jaleo *n.m.* disarray, confusion
jalisco *adj.* stubborn
jamaica *adv.* never
jarana *n.f.* party, entertainment
jetón *n.* boor, idiot
jockey *n.m.* cap, baseball hat
joder *v.* to deceive, screw around with (*infml.*), lie
   to, bother
jote *n.m.* drink of Coke and red wine; patsy (*sl.*)
   (male)
julepe *n.m.* fear
julero *adj.* mendacious

K

kilometraje *n.m.* (significant) experience
kilterry/quilterry *n.* street dog
kiltro/quiltro *n.* street dog, mutt
kinder *n.m.* kindergarten
kino *n.m.* sexual energy; lottery

L

lacho *n.* someone enamored; lecher; womanizer
ladilla *adj.* obnoxious, annoying
ladrillo *n.m.* book (large); unlikeable (person)
lampa *n.* robber
lampiño *adj.* hairless
lana *adj.* hippy-like, laid-back
languí *adj.* hungry
lanza *n.* robber, thief
lanzado *adj.* presumptuous, saucy
lapa *adv., adj.* piggyback
lateado *adj.* bored, disinterested
latero *n.* bore, nuisance
latoso *n.* bore, nuisance
laucha *n.f.* mouse
lauchero *n.m.* cherry-picker (in soccer, *sl.*)
lenteja *adj.* slow, relaxed
lesear *v.* to mock, kid
leseo *n.m.* buffoonery, shenanigans
lesera *n.f.* claptrap, nonsense, banality, triviality
leso *adj.* silly, foolish, clumsy
liceo *n.m.* high school
liebre *n.m.* small bus
ligero/ligerito *adv.* momentarily, shortly
lindorfo *n.m.* bighead, poser, wanna-be hunk
listo *interj.* you're welcome; OK, fine, sure; done
living *n.m.* living room, sofa
liztaylor *adj.* ready
lj *indet.* we left, we went away
loca *n.f.* gal, pal
localidad *n.f.* suburb
loco *n.m.* guy, pal
lola *n.f.* girl
lolo *n.m.* boy
lolosaurio *n.m.* old person who thinks he's young
lomotoro *n.m.* speed bump
longi *adj.* foolish

lorea *interj.* Look!

lorear *v.* to look at, watch

lorenzo *n.* mucus, booger (*sl.*)

loro *n.* chatterbox, talkative person; mucus, booger (*sl.*)

luca *n.f.* 1,000-peso bill

luceros *n.m.pl.* beautiful eyes

lucrecia *n.f.* 1,000-peso bill

lulo *n.m.* long flat bread

luma *n.f.* challenge, strike

lumazo *n.m.* challenge, strike

lumear *v.* to challenge, take on, hit

lunático *adj.* peevish, tempestuous

luquear *v.* to look at

luquiá *n.f.* glance

M

macanuda *adj.* excellent

maceteado *adj.* large, big, muscular

machetear *v.* to beg

machi *n.* witch doctor

machitún *n.m.* herbs

machucao *n.m.* guy

maestro *n.m.* friend, pal

malla *n.f.* string bag

mamadera *n.f.* baby bottle

mamita *n.f.* babe; mother

mamón *n./adj.* fearful; mama's boy

mandao *n.* dominated person (esp. man)

mandonear *v.* to dominate someone

mangi *n.m.* meal

maní *n.* trifle

manjar *n.m.* caramel cream (dulce de leche)

manso *adj.* immense

manyar *v.* to eat

mañoso *adj.* touchy, prickly, irascible

maraca *n.f.* prostitute

matapasión *n.m.* sexual turnoff

matar *v.* to impress, electrify

mate *n.m.* brain; a type of herbal tea

mateo *adj.* studious, intelligent

maula *n.f.* deceit

mazamorra *n.f.* ground corn; hodgepodge

mechero *n.* robber

mechón *n.* first-year college student

mechoneo *n.m.* prank done on first-year college students

medio *adj.* gigantic, huge

meico *n.* witch doctor

menso *adj.* stupid, foolish

menú *n.m.* prix-fixe meal

merme *n.* idiot

merquén *n.m.* ground hot pepper

metalero *n.* heavy metal fanatic

metete *adj.* meddlesome, intrusive

micro *n.m.* local public bus

miércale *interj.* wow!; oh no!

miguelito *n.m.* head of a nail

mijita *n.f.* attractive female (young)

mijito *n.m.* attractive male (young)

milico *n.* military (official)

mino *n.* youth; attractive young person

mocha *n.f.* fight

mojigata *n.f.* imp; someone who pretends to be an angel

mojón *n.m.* excrement

molestar *v.* to rib someone, kid

molestoso *adj.* annoying, pesty

molido *n.m.* loose change

momio *adj.* right-wing

mona *n.f.* fury; hangover

mongo *adj.* foolish, stupid

mono, monito *n.m.* cartoon
moño *n.m.* ponytail
moquillento *adj.* having excessive nasal fluid
moquillento *n.* (*derog.*) youth
mortal *adj.* fantastic, super cool (*sl.*); impressive
mote *n.m.* issue, problem, idea
motel *n.m.* lodging for sex
movida *n.f.* drift (*sl.*), picture (*sl.*)
móvil *n.m.* radio taxi
mula *adj.* false, artificial; bad
mula *n.f.* lie
muletilla *n.f.* crutch (for speaking), meaningless word
municiones *n.pl.* mixed drinks
mutis *adj.* hush-hush

N

nacalapirinaca *interj.* no
nacalapirinaca *n.* nothing
naipe *n.f.* nothing, diddly
nana *n.f.* sister
nanai *n.m.* affection, warmth, caress
nano *n.m.* brother
naranja *n.* nothing
narigona *n.f.* big nose
narizazo *n.m.* big nose
navegado *n.m.* mulled wine
negrero *n.* exploiter, abuser
negro *n.* dark-skinned person
nica *interj.* no way!
nintendo *interj.* no idea, I don't know
nova/toalla nova *n.f.* paper towel
novio *n.* fiancé
numerito *n.m.* scandal
ñegla *adj.* weak

O

oca *adv.* fine, OK
ofri *n.m.* cold
ojudo *n./adj.* big eyes, big-eyed
once *n.f.* light late afternoon meal, teatime
onda *n.f.* niche, segment, clique; energy
oxidar *v.* to sicken (esp. from alcohol)
oyuo *adj.* fortunate

P

p *n.f.* a little, bit
pa' *prep.* to, in order to, for
pachanguear *v.* to have fun, party
pachorro *n.m.* character, charisma
paco *n.m.* (*derog.*) policeman, cop
paila *n.f.* large ear
pailón *n.* big baby (*sl.*)
paja *n.f.* annoyance, shame, boredom
pajarito *n.m.* flake (*sl.*), absentminded (person);
    insect
pajarón *n.* forgetful, spacey
pajeado *adj.* tired, bored
pajero *adj.* lazy
pal *prep.* to, in order to, for
palanquear *v.* to mock, to kid
palanqueo *n.m.* joke
paleta *n.f.* buddy, good guy (*sl.*)
paleteado *adj.* selfless
pálida (la) *n.f.* hangover, groggy feeling
paliducho *adj.* white (esp. face), pale
palo *n.m.* one million pesos
palomita *n.f.* woman
palote *n.* tall person
palta *n.f.* avocado

paltón *n.* wealthy person, high-society person

pan *n.m.* stick (of food, esp. butter)

pana *n.f.* breakdown (car or person), problem, defect

pánfilo *adj.* lazy, lethargic; clumsy

pantis *n.f.pl.* panty hose, stockings

pantruca *n.f.* pallid person; pasta soup

papa *n.f.* hole in clothes; issue, matter; important data; secret; lie; mother's milk

papa *adj.* easy

papaya *adj.* easy

pape *n.m.* slap (esp. on neck)

papeo *n.m.* food

papillón *n.m.* aluminum foil

papillote *n.m.* aluminum foil

papito *n.m.* hunk; father

papú *n.m.* car

papurri *n.* hunk (*sl.*), babe (*sl.*); father; friend

paracaídas *n.f.pl.* uninvited guest

parejito *adj.* tranquil, serene

parte *n.m.* traffic ticket; baptism or wedding invitation

pasamontaña *n.f.* condom

pasar (por) *v.* to stop

pasarse *v.refl.* to do more than enough

pascua *n.f.* Christmas

pasmado *adj.* dim-witted, dense

pasta *n.m.* energy

pastel *n.m.* goofball (*sl.*); dolt; dilemma, difficulty

pasto *n.m.* green vegetables

patear *v.* to boot, kick out of one's life, end a relationship

patero *adj.* ingratiating

patiperrear *v.* to wander, travel

patiperro *n.* travel-lover

pato *n.m.* kiss

pato *adj.* broke, penniless

patojo *n./adj.* short, short person

patota *n.f.* gang, clique, group
patudo *adj.* presumptuous
patudo *n.* large-footed (person)
pavo *adj.* silly, clumsy
paya *n.f.* sung poem
payaya *n.f.* Chilean game
pechar *v.* to mooch
pecosbiles *n.m.pl.* blue jeans
pega *n.f.* job, work, employment
pegado *adj.* preoccupied (with)
pegote *adj.* doting
peineta *adj.* handsome (man), gorgeous
pelado *n.m.* bald person
pelado *adj.* bare, naked
pelador *n.* backstabber, scandalmonger
pelar *v.* to malign, bad-mouth; to rob
película *n.f.* issue, matter
peliento *adj.* coarse, vulgar
pelilargo *adj.* long-haired
pelota *adj.* silly, foolish, disagreeable
pelotera *n.f.* mess, disorder
pelotero *n.* soccer player
pelotudez *n.m.* silliness, stupidity
pelotudo *adj.* dominated (man), idiotic
peludo *adj.* difficult; aged
pelusa *n.* wisecracker, pest
pelusón *adj.* jocular, pesty
penar *v.* to be followed by a spirit
penca *adj.* pathetic, disappointing, lame
penca *n.f.* green celery-like vegetable
pencazo *n.m.* alcoholic drink; kick
pendejada *n.f.* something childish or immature
pendejo *n.* brat; pubic hair
peni *n.m.* penitentiary
penquiarse *v.refl.* to get drunk
peña *n.f.* party, meeting
peñiscar *v.* to pinch

peo/peíto *n.m.* gas, fart

pepa *n.f.* amphetamine; goal (in soccer)

peque *n.* child

perfecto *adj.* right, OK

perfesto *adj.* right, OK

perla *n.* goofball (*sl.*); dolt

perno *n.* dork (*sl.*), geek

perquinazo *adj.* unintelligent

perraje *n.m.* common folk

persa *n.f.* bazaar, flea market

pesado *adj.* ill-tempered, obnoxious, disagreeable

pescar *v.* to pay attention to, listen to

petiso *n./adj.* short; short person

peuca *n.f.* girlfriend, gal, chick, wife

piazo *n.m.* error

picada *n.f.* inexpensive restaurant, thrift store; good idea; good point

picado *adj.* aggrieved, jealous

picaflor *n.m.* womanizer

picanear *v.* insist, pressure, incite

picante *adj.* sleazy, cheesy (*infml.*), coarse

picao, picá *adj.* angry, humorless

picarón *n.m.* womanizer

picarse *v.refl.* to get angry, avenge

pichanga *n.f.* street ("pickup") soccer

pichanguero *n.* soccer player

pichanguiar *v.* to play something (esp. soccer)

pichí *n.m.* urine

pichicatear *v.* to drug, doctor (*sl.*)

pichintún *n.m.* a little, bit

pickle *adj.* vulgar, low class; person who drinks too much

pico *n.m.* little kiss, peck (*infml.*)

picuo *adj.* meddlesome

pierna *n.f.* wife, girlfriend

pifia *n.f.* boo

pifiar *v.* to boo, jeer

pije *adj.* dandy; boorish, ill-mannered
pila *n.f.* group; bunch of fruit or vegetables
pilchas *n.f.pl.* clothes, personal belongings
pilco *n.m.* corn kernels
pililo *adj.* simple, poor
pillería *n.f.* trick
pilucho *adj.* nude
pinchar *v.* to kiss romantically, hook up (*sl.*)
pinche *n.* date; partner
pinga *adj.* vulgar, base
pinganilla *n.* someone vulgar, low-life
pingüino *n.m.* student in uniform
pinochetista *n.* follower of former dictator
    Augusto Pinochet
pinta *n.f.* allure, attractiveness
pintamono *adj.* extroverted; bratty, foolish
pintoso *adj.* appealing, attractive, eye-catching
pinturita *adj.* showy
piñén *n.m.* grime on one's body
piñenienta *n.f.* dirty person
pío *adj.* quiet
piola *adj.* tranquil, quiet, inconspicuous
pipeño *n.m.* cheap wine
pipirisnais *adj.* pretty
piquero *n.m.* dive (in water)
pirigüin *n.f.* water-lover; tadpole, small fish
piruja *adj.* vulgar, sordid
pirulo *adj.* snazzy, dapper
piti *adj.* short-sighted
pitiada *n.f.* puff (of cigarette)
pitiar *v.* to smoke marijuana
pito *n.m.* (marijuana) joint
pituco *adj.* elegant, chic
pitufo *n./adj.* short; short person
pituto *n.m.* contact, connection; temporary work
plancha *n.f.* embarrassment
plantar *v.* to stand someone up (*infml.*)

plata *n.f.* money
po *interj.* emphatic "yes"
pochito *adj.* stuffed, sated
polera *n.f.* t-shirt
polerón *n.m.* sweatshirt
polola *n.f.* girlfriend
pololear *v.* to date
pololeo *n.m.* courting
pololito *n.m.* informal job
pololo *n.m.* boyfriend; womanizer
pomada *n.f.* lie, deception
ponchera *n.f.* beer belly
porfa *interj.* please
porfis *interj.* please
porro *adj.* idle, lazy, uneducated
portaperiódico *n.m.* newspaper holder
posero *n.* poser, wanna-be model
posillo *n.m.* small bowl
posta *n.f.* truth
poto *n.m.* buttocks
prekinder *n.m.* pre-kindergarten
presis *n.m.pl.* presidents
producido *adj.* made-up, cosmetically arranged
pucha *interj.* damn
pucho *n.m.* cigarette
pulenta *n.f.* truth
pulento *adj.* cool, excellent; vulgar
pulpo *n.m.* opportunist; exploiter; bellybutton
puncito *n.m.* gas, fart
punga *adj.* vulgar, bad, thieflike
punta *n.* presumptuous person
puntarelli *n.* presumptuous person
puntear *v.* to stab
puntero *n.* striker (soccer)
puntete *n.m.* kick (soccer)
puntudo *adj.* presumptuous, busybody
puro *adj.* exclusively, only

Q

quaker *n.m.* oatmeal
quebrado *adj.* arrogant, conceited
quebrar *v.* to become arrogant
quedado *adj.* languid
queque *n.m.* sweet bread; buttocks
queridi *adj.* Jewish
queso *n.m.* bind, dilemma
quevedo (*sl.*) *adj.* half-blind, myopic
quina *n.f.* 500 pesos

R

raja *adj.* great, supercool; exhausted; drunk
raja *n.f.* buttocks
rajado *adj.* giving; lucky
rajarse *v.refl.* to luck out; pick up the tab
rajuo *adj.* lucky
ramada *n.f.* place for (independence day) fiestas
rancio *adj.* tired, bored; old
rasca *adj.* sleazy, cheesy, coarse; poor quality
ratero *n.m.* robber
rati *n.m.* police detective
ratón *adj.* insecure, shy; greedy
rayado *adj.* crazy
rayarse *v.refl.* to go crazy
re *adv.* very, quite
rebajoneado *adj.* ill-humored, miserable
regalón *n.* spoiled person
regalonear *v.* to be affectionate, be giving
regio *adj.* fantastic; handsome
reina *n.f.* woman
relajante *adj.* cloyingly sweet
relleno *adj.* fat
remiso *n.* deserter
repetirse *v.refl.* to belch

requetechupete *adj.* excellent
resaca *n.f.* hangover
rescatable *adj.* decent, OK
reventado *adj.* junky, druggish
ricachón *adj.* rich
rico *adj.* attractive, delicious, great
rojelio *adj.* reddened; also used for red
    connotations (e.g., blushing, communist)
rollo *n.m.* difficulty; roll of fat; imagination
roteque *adj.* rude, vulgar
roto *adj.* offensive, discourteous; vulgar, poor,
    low-class
royal *n.m.* baking powder
ruca *n.f.* shack, hut
rucio *adj.* blond
ruler *n.f.* menstruation, period

S

salpica *interj.* leave!, shoo!, beat it!
sapear *v.* to eavesdrop, snoop
sapo *n.* eavesdropper, snoop, gossip
saquero *n.* bad referee
scotch *n.m.* scotch tape
sifri *adv.* yes
sintética *adj.* small-breasted
siútico *adj.* stuck-up
sobaco *n.m.* armpit
sobrado *adj.* arrogant, haughty
socio *n.* friend, pal
solido *adj.* notable, impressive
sonar *v.* to remind of
sopear *v.* to slurp
soplado *adj.* speedy; impeccable
soquete *n.m.* short sock
super *n.m.* supermarket
susodicho *n.* so-and-so

T

tacataca *n.m.* foozball
taco *n.m.* traffic jam
taimao *adj.* sulky, taciturn
taimarse *v.refl.* to clam up (*infml.*)
taita *n.m.* father
talaje *n.m.* beer belly, cattle feed
talla *n.f.* joking, horseplay, silliness
tallado *adj.* crazy
tallero *adj.* funny, entertaining
tambembe *n.m.* buttocks
tapadero *adj.* someone who protects another
    person's lies, someone who covers up
    someone else's wrongdoings
taquillar *v.* to stand out, shine, be noticed; to
    party; to "cruise for chicks"
tarro *n.m.* mouth (big)
tata *n.m.* grandfather, chief
tatequieto *n.m.* punch, slap
tela *n.f.* kind or agreeable person
teléfono *n.m.* telephone number
tete *n.m.* problem, dilemma; pacifier
tevé *n.f.* television
tía *n.f.* affectionate term to refer to older woman
tiernucho *adj.* tender
tincao *n.* fickle person, impulsive or capricious
    person
tincar *v.* to please, appeal to
tintano *n.m.* red wine
tintero *n.* red wine lover
tío *n.m.* affectionate term to refer to older man
tipín *adv.* approximately
tipo *adv.* approximately
tiquitaca *adj.* OK, fine
tira *n.f.* detective
tirado *adj.* alone; rejected (person)

tirar *v.* to kiss; make love

tirarse *v.refl.* to leave quickly, bolt

tocomocho *n.m.* jalopy

toletole *n.m.* quarrel; big mess

tollero *n.* liar, charlatan, pretender

tollo *n.m.* falsehood

tomado *adj.* drunk

tongua *n.* heavy person

torito *n.m.* speed bump

torpedo *n.m.* memory aid, cheat sheet (*sl.*)

torrante *adj.* lazy, low class, destitute

torreja *adj.* vulgar, base

totué *n.m.* magic bird

tóxico *adj.* disagreeable, yucky (*sl.*), stinky

toyento *adj.* loquacious

toyo *n.m.* malarkey

tranca *n.f.* mental problem, hangover

trancailla *n.f.* trip-up

tronco *adj.* stiff

troncomovil *n.m.* car

trutro *n.m.* chicken thigh

tufo *n.m.* breath (esp. bad)

tumba *n.* secret keeper

turco *n.* Arab

turro *n.m.* stack (esp. of bills)

tuto *n.m.* sleep, fatigue; chicken thigh; baby's blanket

tutti *n.m.* everything

U

ubicar *v.* to know, be familiar with

ubicarse *v.refl.* to behave (oneself)

ulceroso *adj.* ill-humored

ulpo *adj.* stupid, foolish, boring

ulpo *n.m.* drink of toasted flour, hot water, and sugar

último *adj.* terrible, awful
unto *n.m.* animal fat
upeliento *adj.* Allendistas (supporters of President
    Salvador Allende)
urgidor *adj.* bossy, nagging
uslero *n.m.* rolling pin

V

vaca *n.f.* collection of money; fatso; traitor
vacuna *n.* traitor, bad person
vale *n.m.* receipt
veep *n.m.* VIP (very important person)
vejestorio *adj.* antiquated
venado *n.m.* person cheated on
vieja *n.f.* mother, female friend, friend's mother
viejo *n.m.* father
viejujo *n.m.* old man; dirty old man
virarse *v.refl.* to leave
visagra *n.f.* knee
volado *adj.* flaky (*sl.*), spacey (*sl.*); drugged
volar *v.* to go out, leave; to be drugged, be stoned

Y

ya *interj.* yes, OK, right
yapa *n.f.* small gift
yastá *adj.* OK, fine
yaya *n.f.* cut, wound
yegua *n.f.* bitch (*sl.*, *derog.*)
yeta *n.* unlucky person
yunta *n.f.* pair, couple
yuta *n.f.* paddy wagon

Z

zapallo *n.m.* head
zarpar *v.* to leave, go away
zeta *adj.* asleep
zorra *n.f.* madhouse, mess; woman (*derog.*)
zota *n.f.* ten-peso coin

English-Chilenismos Dictionary

A

ability *n.* cachaña *f.*
accumulate *v.* achoclonar
affection *n.* nanai *m.*
aged *adj.* peludo
aggrieved *adj.* picado
agitator *n.* carbonero
alcoholic drink *n.* copete *m.*, pencazo *m.*
alga *n.* huiro *m.*
Allende supporter *adj.* upeliento
allure *n.* pinta *f.*
alone *adj.* tirado
also *adv.* igual
aluminum foil *n.* papillón *m.*, papillote *m.*
amphetamine *n.* pepa *f.*
and *adv.* igual
anger *v.* achorarse, empelotarse, enyegüecer,
   amurrarse, picarse, emplumarse
anger *n.* bronca *f.*
angry *adj.* choreado, emputecido, enajenado,
   envenado, picao, picá, empelotado
annoyance *n.* paja *f.*
annoying *adj.* camote, molestoso, aguja
antiquated *adj.* vejestorio
anyway *adv.* igual
apathetic *adj.* funado
appeal to *v.* tincar
appealing *adj.* pintoso

approximately *adv.* tipín, tipo
Arab *n.* turco
armpit *n.* sobaco *m.*
arrogant *adj.* inflado, cachetón, quebrado, sobrado
artificial *adj.* mula *f.*
ashamed *adj.* achunchado
Asian (features) *adj.* chino
Asian *n.* chino
askew *adj.* cuneteado
asleep *adj.* zeta
assailant *n.* cogotero
assault *v.* cogotear
at once *adv.* altirante, altiro
attached *adj.* agarrado
attachment *n.* attach *m.*
attention-seeker *n.* figurón
attractive *adj.* pintoso, rico, carnudo, cachilupi
attractive (person) *n.* mijito *m.*, mijita *f.*, guachito *m.*, guachita *f.*
attractiveness *n.* pinta *f.*
Augusto Pinochet supporter *n.* pinochetista
auto (old) *n.* cacharro *m.*
avocado *n.* palta *f.*
awesome *adj.* bacán
awful *adj.* último
awry *adj.* cuneteado

B

babe (*sl.*) *n.* bomba, mamita, papurri
baby *n.* guagua
babylike *n.* guagualón
backstabber *n.* pelador
backtrack *v.* achaplinarse
bad *adj.* charcho, mula

bad breath *n.* tufo *m.*
bad guy *n.* choro
bad luck *n.* funa *f.*
bad-mouth *v.* pelar
bad referee *n.* saquero
bag (paper) *n.* cambucho *m.*
bag (string) *n.* malla *f.*
baking powder *n.* royal *m.*
bald person *n.* pelado *m.*
banality *n.* lesera *f.*
bare *adj.* pelado
base *adj.* torreja, pinganilla
bathroom *n.* guater *m.*
bazaar *n.* persa *f.*
be giving *v.* regalonear
be right *v.* achuntar
be unfaithful *v.* gorrear, cagar
beautiful *adj.* flor
beauty *n.* filete
become aroused *v.* enyegüecer
become arrogant *v.* quebrar
become frightened *v.* arratonarse
beer *n.* chela, chelita *f.*
beer belly *(sl.)* *n.* ponchera *f.*, talaje *m.*
beg *v.* machetear
behave (oneself) *v.refl.* ubicarse
belch *v.* repetirse
belly *n.* guata *f.*
bellybutton *n.* pulpo *m.*
belt *n.* guasca *f.*
bicycle *n.* cleta *f.*
big *adj.* maceteado
big baby *(sl.)* *n.* pailón
big eyes *n.* ojudo
big girl *n.* grandota *f.*
big guy *n.* grandote *m.*
big mouth *n.* hocicón, bocón

big nose *n.* narigona *f.*, narizazo *m.*
bighead *n.* lindorfo *m.*
bind *n.* queso *m.*
bird (magic) *n.* totué *m.*
bit *n. f.*, pichintún *m.*
bitch (*sl.*, *derog.*) *n.* yegua *f.*
blabbermouth *n.* hocicón, gritón, bocón
blanket (for baby) *n.* tuto *m.*
blond *adj.* rucio
blow (hit) *n.* cachuchazo *m.*
blue jeans *n.pl.* bluyines *m.*, pecosbiles *m.*
boast *v.* cachiporrearse
bold *adj.* choro
bolt (*sl.*) *v.* tirarse
boo *n.* pifia *f.*
boo *v.* pifiar
booger (*sl.*) *n.* lorenzo *m.*
book *n.* ladrillo *m.*
boor *n.* jetón
boorish *adj.* pije
boot (from one's life) *v.* patear
boozer *n.* chicha *f.*
bore *n.* latero, latoso
bored *adj.* lateado, pajeado
boredom *n.* fomedad *f.*, paja *f.*
boring *adj.* fome, fomeque
bossy *adj.* urgidor
bother *v.* catetear, hinchar
bottle (baby) *n.* mamadera *f.*
bowl (small) *n.* posillo *m.*
bowl *n.* impote *m.*
boy *n.* cachorro, cabro *m.*
boyfriend *n.* pololo *m.*
braggart *adj.* cachiporra
brain *n.* mate *m.*
brat *n.* pendejo
bratty *adj.* pintamono

bread *n.* doblada *f.*, hallulla *f.*, lulo *m.*

break down *v.* chacrearse, chispotear, clotear, funarse

breakdown *n.* pana *f.*

breath (esp. bad) *n.* foca *f.*, tufo *m.*

broke *adj.* calato, pato, cinco

brother *n.* nano *m.*

brutal *adj.* bikingo

buddy *n.* gancho, güeón, maestro, socio, paleta *f.*, flaco

buffoonery *n.* chacoteo *m.*, güeveo *m.*, leceo *m.*, chingana *f.*

bug *v.* catetear

bumpkin *n.* huaso

bunkbed *n.* camarote *m.*

burning up *adj.* cocido

burp *n.* chancho *m.*

bus (local) *n.* micro *m.*, liebre (small) *m.*, guagua *f.*

bushy hair *n.* champa *f.*

butch *adj.* amachada

buttocks *n.* poto *m.*, tambembe *m.*, queque *m.*, raja *f.*

C

cafeteria *n.* casino *m.*

can (*sl.* for jail) *n.* cana *f.*

cap *n.* jockey *m.*

car *n.* troncomovil *m.*, papú *m.*

caramel (candy) *n.* caluga *f.*

caramel (cream, dulce de leche) *n.* manjar *m.*

carouse *v.* carretear

cartoon *n.* mono, monito *m.*

challenge *n.* luma *f.*

challenge *v.* lumear

challenging *adj.* complicado

change (loose) *n.* molido *m.*
change purse *n.* choro *m.*
character (*sl.*) *n.* chacotero
charisma *n.* pachorro *m.*
charlatan *n.* tollero
chat *v.* chotorrear
chatterbox *n.* loro *m.*, toyento
cheap *adj.* botado
cheap wine *n.* pipeño *m.*
cheated upon *adj.* cuernúo
cheat sheet (*sl.*) *n.* torpedo *m.*
cheeky *adj.* barsa, fresco
cherry-picker (in soccer) *n.* lauchero *m.*
chic *adj.* pituco
chick (*sl.*) *n.* cachorra, cabra *f.*
chicken thigh *n.* tuto, trutro *m.*
chief *n.* tata *m.*
child *n.* peque
childish *adj.* alolado
Chilean game *n.* payaya *f.*
chin *n.* pera *f.*
chintzy *adj.* cagado
choked *adj.* abutagado
Christmas *n.* pascua *f.*
chug *v.* empinar
cider (hard) *n.* chicha *f.*, chupilca *f.*
cigarette *n.* pucho *m.*
city person *n.* citadino *m.*
clam up *v.* taimarse
claptrap *n.* lesera *f.*
clever *adj.* caperuzo
clique *n.* patota *f.*
clogged *adj.* abutagado
cloth *n.* chiteco *m.*
clothes *n.* pilchas *f.pl.*

cloying *adj.* relajante
clumsy *adj.* leso, pánfilo, burra, pao
coal shards *n.* cijo *m.*
coarse *adj.* guachaca, peliento
cold *n.* ofri *m.*
collection (money) *n.* vaca *f.*
common folk *n.* perraje *m.*
communist *n.* comunacho *m.*
complicated *adj.* atadoso, fregado
complication *n.* atado *m.*
compliment *n.* chirola *m.*
computer geek *n.* computín, ina
conceited *adj.* agrandado, quebrado
confusion *n.* jaleo *m.*
connection *n.* pituto *m.*
contact *n.* pituto *m.*
content *adj.* chocho, embalado
converse *v.* chacharear
cool (*sl.*) *adj.* bacán, chacal, pulento, heavy
cop *n.* paco (*derog.*)
copycat *n.* copión *m.*
corn kernels *n.* pilco *m.*
corrupt *adj.* chueco
cosmetically arranged *adj.* producido
couple *n.* yunta *f.*
courting *n.* pololeo *m.*
cowardly *adj.* arranado
crazy *adj.* rayado, tallado
crazy (person) *n.* chucheta
croak *n.* gallito *m.*
crowd-pleaser *n.* pintamono
crutch (*sl.*) *n.* muletilla *f.*
cup (of wine) *n.* caña *f.*
curl (of hair) *n.* chocho *m.*
custom *n.* enchapado *m.*
cut *n.* yaya *f.*

D

dad *n.* viejo *m.*
dance (national) *n.* cueca *f.*
dapper *adj.* empaquetado, emperifollado, pirulo
dark-skinned *n.* negro
darn *interj.* ¡chupalla!, ¡conchalevale!
data *n.* papa *f.*
date (person) *v.* pololear
date (person) *n.* pinche
daughter *n.f.* chicoca
dear *n.* cosita *f.*
deceit *n.* maula *f.*
deceived *adj.* cuernúo
decent *adj.* rescatable
deception *n.* grupo *m.* (circulo de amigos)
defect *n.* pana *f.*
delicate *adj.* cursi
delicious *adj.* rico
delinquent *n.* choro
dense *adj.* pasmado, brígido
depreciate *v.* chacrearse
depressed *adj.* bajoneado
depression *n.* depre *f.*
deserter *n.* remiso
destitute *adj.* torrante
detective *n.* rati *m.*, tira *f.*
diddly *n.* callampa *f.*, hongo *m.*, maní *m.*
difficult *adj.* cototo, fregado, peludo
difficulty *n.* rollo *m.*, pastel *m.*
diffident *adj.* cartucho
dilemma *n.* cacho *m.*, tete *m.*, forro *m.*, pastel *m.*
dim-witted *adj.* asopado, pasmado, durazno
dirty *v.* churretear
dirty (person) *n.* piñenienta
dirty *adj.* churreteado
disagreeable *adj.* pesado, brígido, fregado

disarray *n.* jaleo *m.*

discarded (person) *adj.* tirado, botado

discourteous *adj.* roto

disingenuous *adj.* cartucho

disinterested *adj.* lateado

disobedient *adj.* cascarrabias

disorder *n.* despelote *m.*, pelotera *f.*

dispute *n.* encontrón *m.*

disrobe *v.* empilucharse, empelotarse

distant *prep.* chuchunco

dive (in water) *n.* piquero *m.*

dolt *n.* güeón, perla, pastel

dominate (someone) *v.* mandonear

dominated (man) *adj.* pelotudo, mandao

done *interj.* chao, listo

doomed *adj.* cagado, frito

dork (*sl.*) *n.* perno

doting *adj.* pegote, estampilla, chape

doubtful *n.* cachuo *m.*

dough (*sl.* money) *n.* chaucha *m.*

drift (*sl.*) *n.* movida *f.*

drink (heavily) *v.* curarse

drink (mixed) *n.* municiones *pl.*

drudge *n.* goma

drug *v.* pichicatear

drugged *adj.* doblado, volado

druggish *adj.* reventado

drunk *adj.* curado, cocido, botado, tomado, doblado, copeteado

drunk *n.* cucarro, guaripoleao

E

ear (large) *n.* paila *f.*

easy *adj.* papaya, papa

eat *v.* manyar

eavesdrop *v.* sapear
eavesdropper *n.* sapo
egoistic *adj.* amarrete
electrify matar *v.*
elegant *adj.* pituco
elementary school *n.* colegio *m.*
email *n.* emilio *m.*
embarrassed *adj.* arranado
embarrassment *n.* plancha *f.*
employment *n.* pega *f.*
end *v.* funarse
energy *n.* pasta *m.*, onda *f.*
energy (sexual) *n.* kino *m.*
entertaining *adj.* tallero, cachilupi, chori
entertainment *n.* jarana *f.*
enthuse *v.* entrar
err *v.* embarrar
error *n.* condoro *m.*, piazo *m.*
evangelical *adj.* canuto
everything *n.* tutti *m.*
exaggerated *adj.* coloriento, alaraco, cuático
exaggeration *n.* color *m.*
exceedingly *adv.* demás
excellent *adj.* choro, macanuda, requetechupete,
  benaiga, pulento, cototo
exclusively *adj.* puro
excrement *n.* mojón *m.*
execute (esp. sports) *v.* chantar
exhausted *adj.* raja
experience *n.* kilometraje *m.*
expert *n.* cabrón
expletive *n.* garabato *m.*
exploitative *adj.* fresco
exploiter *n.* negrero, cafiche, pulpo *m.*
extrovert *n.* pintamono
eye (big) *n.* ojudo
eye-catching *adj.* pintoso
eyes (beautiful) *n.pl.* luceros (*m.pl.*)

F

fabrication *n.* chiva *f.*
fake *adj.* chanta, mula
false *adj.* chanta, mula
falsehood *n.* tollo *m.*
fans *n.pl.* barra
fantastic *adj.* regio, benaiga, mortal, caballo, groso, heavy
far *prep.* chuchunco
fart *n.* peo/peíto, puncito *m.*
fat *adj.* relleno, guatón
fat (animal) *n.* unto *m.*
father *n.* taita, papurri, viejo *m.*
fatigue *n.* tuto *m.*
fatso *n.* flotador, bola de grasa, guatón
favor *n.* gauchada *f.*
fear *n.* julepe *m.*
fearful *adj.* mamón
fearless *adj.* choro
fed up *adj.* cabreado, apestado
fickle (person) *n.* tincao
fiery (person) *n.* indio
fight *n.* encontrón *m.*, mocha *f.*
fighter *n.* chúcaro
filthy *adj.* cochino
fine *adj.* yastá, tiquitaca, flor, oca
finicky *adj.* exquisito
finished *interj.* chao
five hundred pesos *n.* quina *f.*
five thousand peso bill *n.* gabriela *f.*
flake (*sl.*) *n.* pajarito *m.*
flaky (*sl.*) *adj.* volado
flip-flop (shoe) *n.* hawaiana *f.*
flirtatious *adj.* coco roco
foolish (person) *n.* jote *m.*

food *n.* papeo *m.*

foolish *adj.* ganso, longi, asopado, gilberto, mongo, menso, pelota

foolishness *n.* güeveo *m.*

foot *n.* gamba *f.*

foozball *n.* tacataca *m.*

for *prep.* pal, pa'

foreign (Western) *adj.* agringado

forget *v.* chipotearse

forgetful *n.* pajarón

formally-dressed *adj.* empaquetado

fortunate *adj.* oyuo

French *n./adj.* franchute

fried food *n.* fritanga *f.*

friend (older) *n.* tío, tía

friend *n.* gancho, güeón, maestro, socio, vieja, papurri, chato

fun *adj.* chori

funny *adj.* tallero

furious *adj.* emputecido

fury *n.* mona *f.*

G

gal *n.* comadre, galla, gansa, loca

gang *n.* patota *f.*

gas *n.* peo/peíto, puncito *m.*

gas station *n.* bomba *f.*

geek (*sl.*) *n.* perno

get by *v.* defenderse

get drunk *v.* penquiarse

get hot *v.* caldiarse

get lost *v.* garetearse

get on *v.* encaramar

gift *n.* engañito *m.*, yapa *f.*

gigantic *adj.* medio

girl *n.* cachorra, cabra *f.*
girlfriend *n.* pierna, polola, peuca *f.*
giving *adj.* rajado
glance *n.* luquiá *f.*
glutton *n.* agarraguire
go batty (*sl.*) *v.* enyegüecer
go crazy *v.* rayarse
go up *v.* encaramar
goal (soccer) *n.* pepa *f.*
good *adj.* cachilupi
good-bye *interj.* chavela
good guy (*sl.*) *n.* paleta *f.*
goof around *v.* farrear
goofball *n.* perla
gorgeous *adj.* encachao
gossip *n.* sapo *m.*
grandfather *n.* tata *m.*
great *adj.* chacal, rico, raja, güendy
greedy *adj.* amarrete, coñete, ratón, angurriento
grime *n.* piñén *m.*
gringo-like *adj.* agringado
ground corn *n.* mazamorra *f.*
group *n.* patota *f.*, pila (of vegetables, etc.) *f.*
guest (uninvited) *n.* paracaídas *f.pl.*
guy *n.* gallo, ganso, loco, machucao *m.*

H

habit *n.* enchapado *m.*
ha-ha-ha *interj.* jajaja
hairless *adj.* lampiño
half-blind (*sl.*) *adj.* quevedo
handsome *adj.* regio, carnudo, encachao, peineta
hang out (with thugs) *v.* chuliar
hangover *n.* hachazo *f.*, resaca *f.*, pálida, caña *f.*,
    mona *f.*

happy *adj.* chocho
hard cider *n.* chicha *f.*, chupilca *f.*
hat *n.* chupalla *f.*
haughty *adj.* sobrado
have fun *v.* pachanguear
head *n.* zapallo *m.*
heavy metal fanatic *n.* metalero
heavy person *n.* tongua
heed *v.* enganchar, inflar
herbal tea *n.* mate *m.*
herbs *n.pl.* machitún
here *adv.* acato
hide *v.* fondear
high school *n.m.* liceo
hippy *n.* artesa
hippy-like *adj.* lana
hit *n.* cachuchazo *m.*, guascazo *m.*, fleta *f.*
hit *v.* fletar
hoarder *adj.* buche
hodgepodge *n.* mazamorra *f.*
hole (in clothes) *n.* papa *f.*
hook up (*sl.*) *v.* atinar
hookey (*sl.*) *n.* cimarra *f.*
hooligans *n.pl.* barra brava
horizontal *adj.* asolío
horny (*sl.*) *adj.* califa, castizo, cachero
horseplay *n.* talla *f.*
hot *adj.* caldiao
hot pepper (ground) *n.* merquén *m.*
huge *adj.* medio
humorless *adj.* picao, picá
hungover *adj.* copeteado
hungry *adj.* angurriento, gasuso, languí
hunk *n.* guachito, papito, papurri
hurry *v.* chicotear
hush-hush *adj.* muti
hut *n.* ruca *f.*

I

idea *n.* mote *m.*
idiot *n.* merme, jetón
idiotic *adj.* pelotudo, güehéta
ill-humored *adj.* denso, rebajoneado, ulceroso
ill-mannered *adj.* pije
ill-tempered *adj.* pesado
imagination *n.* rollo *m.*
immature (person) *n.* pendejada
immediately *adv.* altirante, altiro
immense *adj.* manso
imp *n.* mojigata *f.*
impeccable *adj.* soplado, impeque
importunate *adj.* aguja
impress *v.* matar
impressive *adj.* sólido
incompetent *adj.* amermelado
inconspicuous *adj.* piola
indebted *adj.* encalillado
inexpensive *adj.* botado
infantile *adj.* aguaguada
infatuated *adj.* enyegüesido
inflexible *adj.* acartonado
ingratiating *adj.* patero
innumerable *adj.* cualquier
insect *n.* pajarito *m.*
insecure *adj.* ratón
insist *v.* picanear
insistent *adj.* catete, cargante
instinct *n.* cachativa *f.*
intelligent *adj.* mateo, capo
intrusive *adj.* metete
intuition *n.* cachativa *f.*
invitation (esp. baptism, wedding) *n.* parte *m.*
involved *adj.* enrollado
ire *n.* bronca *f.*
issue *n.* papa *f.*, película *f.*, mote *m.*, guarifafa *f.*

J

jail *n.* cana *f.*
jealous *adj.* picado
jeer *v.* pifiar
jello *n.* jalea *f.*
jerk *n.* güeón
Jewish *adj.* queridi
jilt *v.* chutear
job *n.* pega *f.*, pololito *m.*
jocular *adj.* pelusón
joint (marijuana) *n.* huiro *m.*, pito *m.*, marciano *m.*,
     cuete *m.*
joke *n.* palanqueo *m.*
joker *n.* chacotero
juicy *adj.* caldúo
junk *n.* cachureo *m.*
junk food *n.* chatarra *f.*
junky *adj.* reventado

K

kick (soccer) *n.* puntete *m.*, pencazo *m.*
kick *v.* chutear
kid *v.* güevear, lesear, palanquear, molestar
kill *v.* funar
kind (person) *n.* tela *f.*
kindergarten *n.* kinder *m.*
kiss *v.* pinchar, atracar, agarrar, atinar, tirar
kiss *n.* atraque *m.*, (little) pico, piquito *m.*
kiss *n.* pato *m.*
knee *n.* visagra *f.*
knick-knack *n.* cachureo *m.*
knockout *n.* guachita
know-it-all *adj.* jalisco

L

lad *n.* cachorro, cabro *m.*
ladybug *n.* chinita *f.*
laid-back *adj.* lana, flopy
lame *adj.* fome, fomeque, penca
lameness *n.* fomedad *f.*
languid *adj.* quedado
large *adj.* maceteado
larger-than-life *adj.* cuático
laze *v.* flojear
lazy *adj.* pánfilo, porro, pajero
leave *v.* virarse, volar, zarpar
lecher *n.* lacho
lethargic *adj.* pánfilo
liar *n.* chiviento, tollero, cahuinero
liberate *v.* descartuchar
lie *n.* grupo *m.*, chiva *f.*, cahuín *m.*, papa *f.*,
    pomada *f.*, mula *f.*
lie *v.* engrupir
likewise *adv.* escoba
little *n.* pichintún *m.*
livid *adj.* empelotado, emputecido
living room *n.* living *m.*
loaded (rich) (*sl.*) *adj.* cargado
lodging (for sex) *n.* motel *m.*
long face (*infml.*) *n.* caracho *m.*
long-haired *adj.* pelilargo
look *v.* catear
look at *v.* luquear, lorear
loquacious *adj.* chachero, toyento
lots *adv.* caleta, ene, cualquier
lottery *n.* kino *m.*
lounge *v.* flojear
love (in love) *adj.* enganchao, agarrado
low-class *adj.* guachaca

lower *v.* bajonear
low-life (person) *n.* pinganilla
low-life *adj.* chihua
luck *n.* cuea *f.*
luck (out) *v.refl.* rajarse
lucky *adj.* cueuo, rajado, rajuo

M

madhouse *n.* zorra *f.*
magnificently *adv.* descueve
make love *v.* tirar
malarkey *n.* toyo *m.*, chácara *f.* (cuento para distraer)
malign *v.* descuerar, cahuinear, pelar
man (dominated) *n.* calzonero *m.*
man (old/dirty) *n.* viejujo *m.*
many *adv.* ene
marijuana *n.* ganga *f.*
market *n.* persa *f.*
matter *n.* asunteque *m.*
meal *n.* mangi *m.*
meal (light, late afternoon; teatime) *n.* once *f.*
meaningless word *n.* muletilla *f.*
meddlesome *adj.* metete, picuo
meeting *n.* peña *f.*
memory aid *n.* torpedo *m.*
mendacious *adj.* grupiento, julero, chanta
menstruation *n.* ruler *f.*
mental problem *n.* tranca *f.*
mess *n.* pelotera *f.*, zorra *f.*
messy *adj.* destartalado
military (official) *n.* milico
milk (mother's) *n.* papa *f.*
miserable *adj.* rebajoneado
miss (young girl) *n.* casera

mistake *n.* condoro *m.*

mock *v.* güevear, lesear, palanquear, columpiar

mockery *n.* huichicheo *m.*

moment *n.* cachito *m.*

momentarily *adv.* ligero, ligerito, altiro, altirante

money *n.* billullo *m.*, plata *f.*, chaucha *m.*

mooch *v.* bolsear, pechar

mooch *n./adj.* bolsero

mother *n.* mamita *f.*, vieja *f.*

mouse *n.* laucha *f.*

mouth *n.* tarro *m.*, (big) hocico

mucus *n.* loro *m.*

multitude *n.* chorrera *f.*

muscular *adj.* maceteado

mussel *n.* choro *m.*

N

nagging *adj.* urgidor

nail (head) *n.* miguelito *m.*

naked *adj.* pelado

nasal fluid (excessive) *adj.* moquillento

natty *adj.* empaquetado

neck *n.* cogote *m.*

neckless *adj.* cinco

never *adv.* jamaica

newspaper holder *n.* portaperiódico *m.*

nice *adj.* dije

niche *n.* onda *f.*

no *interj.* nacalapirinaca

no idea *interj.* nintendo

no matter *interj.* filo

no way *interj.* nica

noble *n.* jaibón

nosy *adj.* copuchento
nothing *n.* callampa, hongo, naiper, nacalapirinaca, naranja
nude *adj.* pilucho, calato
nuisance *n.* latero, latoso

O

oatmeal *n.* quaker *m.*
obnoxious *adj.* pesado, camote, ladilla
obsess *v.* enrollarse
offensive *adj.* roto, roteque
OK *adj.* oca, rescatable, yastá, tiquitaca, perfecto, perfesto
OK *adv.* ya, listo
old *adj.* rancio
one hundred pesos *n.* gamba *f.*
one million pesos *n.* palo *m.*
one million pesos *n.* guaton *m.*
one thousand peso bill *n.* luca *f.*, lucrecia *f.*
only *adj.* puro
opportunist *n.* pulpo *m.*
optimistic *adj.* aperrado
orphan *n.* guacho *m.*
outdo (oneself) (*sl.*) *v.refl.* pasarse
overambitious *adj.* coñete
owl *n.* chuncho *m.*

P

pacifier *n.* tete *f.*
pack *n.* gallada *f.*
paddy wagon *n.* yuta *f.*
pained *adj.* achacado
pair *n.* yunta *f.*

pal *n.* compadre, flaco, chato
pallid (person) *n.* pantruca
pamper *v.* aguachar
panty hose *n.* pantis *f.pl.*
paper bag *n.* cambucho *m.*
paper towel *n.* nova *f.*
partner *n.* pinche
party *v.* carretear, taquillar
party *n.* canyengue *f.*, chingana *f.*, peña *f.*, jarana *f.*
party animal (*sl.*) *n.* carretero
pathetic *adj.* fome, fomeque, penca
patsy (*sl.*) *n.* jote *m.*
pay (whole tab) *v.* rajarse
pay attention (to) *v.* pescar, enganchar
peach *n.* durazno *m.*
peevish *adj.* lunático
penitentiary *n.* peni *m.*
perhaps *adv.* capaz
period (menstruation) *n.* ruler *f.*
personage *n.* artista
personal belongings *n.* pilchas *f.pl.*
pest *n.* pelusa
pesty *adj.* molestoso, pelusón
phlegm *n.* desgarro *m.*
piggyback *adv.*, *adj.* lapa, a nacha
pile up *v.* achoclonar
pimple *n.* espornocu *m.*
pinch *v.* peñiscar
Pisco-and-soda *n.* combinado *m.*
place for parties *n.* ramada *f.*, fonda *f.*
play (esp. soccer) *v.* pichanguiar
please *interj.* porfa, porfis
please *v.* tincar
poem (sung) *n.* paya *f.*
point (argument) *n.* picada *f.*
policeman *n.* paco (*derog.*)
polite *adj.* dije

ponytail *n.m.* moño
poor *adj.* pililo, roto, guachaca
popcorn *n.* cabrita *f.pl.*
poser *n.* lindorfo, posero
pot (large) *n.* fondo *m.*
prekindergarten *n.* prekinder *m.* jardín *m.*
preoccupied (with) *adj.* pegado (a)
presidents *n.m.* presis
pressure *v.* picanear
presumptuous *adj.* patudo, puntudo, blasa, lanzado
presumptuous (person) *n.* punta, puntarelli
pretender *n.* tollero
pretty *adj.* pipirisnais
prickly *adj.* mañoso
prisoner *n.* canero
prix-fixe meal *n.* menú *m.*
problem *n.* atado *m.*, cacho *m.*, tete *m.*, mote *m.*,
     guarifafa *f.*, pana *f.*
problematic *adj.* atadoso
prostitute *n.* maraca *f.*
proud *adj* chocho
provide *v.* aperarse
prying *adj.* copuchento
pubic hair *n.* pendejo
puff (of cigarette) *n.* pitiada *f.*
punch *n.* combo *m.*, tatequieto *m.*
punk *n.* güeón
pushover *n.* guerrera *f.*

Q

quarrel *n.* toletole *m.*
quick-witted *adj.* aguja
quiet *adj.* piola
quite *adv.* re
quiz *n.* control *m.*

R

rabble-rouser *n.* carbonero
radio taxi *n.* movíl *m.*
ready *adj.* liztaylor
rebel *n.* chúcaro
receipt *n.* vale *m.*
recently *adv.* denante
reddened *adj.* rojelio
red wine *n.* tintano *m.*
red wine lover *n.* tintero
red-head *n.* fanta *f.*
refrigerator *n.* frigider *m.*
rejected *adj.* botado
rejoin *v.* enchufarse
relaxed *adj.* lenteja, flopy
remind (of) *v.* sonar
repent *v.* arratonarse, achaplinarse
reserved *adj.* cartucho
resilient *adj.* aperrado
rev (a car) *v.* aserruchar
reveler *n.* carretero
revelry *n.* carrete *m.*
rib *v.* molestar
rich *adj.* ricachón, high
right *interj.* ya, listo
right *adj.* perfecto, perfesto
right-wing *adj.* momio
right-winger *n.* facho
rigid *adj.* acartonado
rob *v.* pelar
robber *n.* güiiña, ratero, lanza, lampa, mechero
Rock, Paper, Scissors (hand game) *n.* cachipún *m.*
roll (of fat) *n.* rollo *m.*
rolling pin *n.* uslero *m.*
rowdy person *n.* chucheta

ruin *v.* embarrar
rumor *n.* cahuín *m.*
rumormonger *n.* cahuinero

S

sad *adj.* bajoneado, achacado, decaído
sandal *n.* chala *f.*
sassy *adj.* fresco
sated *adj.* chato, pochito
saucy *adj.* lanzado
scab *n.* caracha
scandal *n.* numerito *m.*
scandalmonger *n.* pelador
secret *n.* papa *f.*
secret keeper *n.* tumba
see *v.* cachar
selfless *adj.* paleteado
serene *adj.* parejito
serious *adj.* fregado
shame *n.* paja *f.*
shameless *adj.* barsa
shantytown *n.* callampa *f.*
sharp-dresser *n.m.* facha
shenanigans *n.pl.* chacoteo *m.*, güeveo *m.*, leceo *m.*
short *adj.* choco, patojo, pitufo, petiso
shortly *adv.* ligero, ligerito
short person *n.* choco, patojo, pitufo, petiso
short-sighted *adj.* piti
shoulder (road) *n.* berma *f.*
shower faucet (detachable) *n.* ducha teléfono *f.*
show-stealing *adj.* cuático
showy *adj.* florerito, pinturita
shriek (childish) *interj.* huichipirichi
sick *adj.* decaído
sicken (usu. alcohol) *v.* oxidar
side (of buttocks) *n.* cachete *m.*

silliness *n.* talla *f.*, pelotudez *m.*
silly *adj.* burra, perno, agilado, gilberto
simple *adj.* pililo, botado
sir *n.* casero
sister *n.* nana *f.*
skill *n.* cachaña *f.*
slab (of wood) *n.* choco *m.*
slap *n.* tatequieto *m.*, fleta *f.*
slap (playful) *n.* camotera *f.*, pape *m.*
slavish *adj.* arrastrado
sleazy *adj.* cebollento, picante, rasca, chulo
sleep *n.* tuto *m.*
slimy (person) *adj.* chulo
slipper *n.* bachata *f.*, chalupa *f.*
slow *adj.* lenteja
slurp *v.* sopear
smart *adj.* caperuzo
smitten *adj.* embalado, enganchao, enyegüesido
smoke (marijuana) *v.* pitiar
smoker (heavy) *n.* chimenea *f.*
smooch *n.* calugazo *m.*
snack *n.* choca, choquita *f.*
snazzy *adj.* pirulo
snoop *n.* sapo
snoop *v.* sapear
snort (drugs) *v.* jalar
so-and-so *n.* susodicho
soap opera fan (male) *n.* calzonero *m.*
soccer (pickup game) *n.* pichanga *f.*
soccer player *n.* pelotero, pichanguero
sock *n.m.* soquete
soda *n.* bebida *f.*
solitary *adj.* botella
sour on *v.* achacar
spacey (*sl.*) *adj.* volado
speed bump *n.* lomotoro *m.*, torito *m.*
speedy *adj.* soplado
spirit *n.* bicho *m.*

spittle *n.* gargajo *m.*

spoil (oneself) *v.refl.* castigarse

spoiled (person) *n.* regalón

spoiled (person) *adj.* regalón, aguaguado

stab *v.* puntear

stack (esp. of bills) *n.* turro

stand out *v.* taquillar

stand up (*sl.*) *v.* plantar

steal *v.* chorrear

stick (e.g., of butter) *n.* pan *m.*

stiff *adj.* tronco

stingy *adj.*carqueta, coñete, apretado

stinky *adj.* tóxico

stomach *n.* guata *f.*

stomach muscle *n.* caluga *f.*

stop (by) *v.* pasar (por)

store (small) *n.* boliche *m.*

store (inexpensive) *n.* picada *f.*

strap *n.* guasca *f.*

strawberry *n.* frutilla *f.*

street dog *n.* kiltro/quiltro *m.*, kilterry/quilterry *m.*

street talk *n.* coa *f.*

strict *adj.* fregado

strike *n.* lumazo *m.*

striker (soccer) *n.* puntero

strong *adj.* aliñado

stubborn *adj.* jalisco, cascarrabias, catete, durazno

stuck-up *adj.* siútico

stud (*sl.*) *n.* canchero

student *n.* canario, pingüino, mechón

studious *adj.* ateo

stuffed *adj.* chato, pochito

stupid *adj.* agüeonado, pao, gil, ganso, mongo, ulpo

stupidity *n.* pelotudez *m.*, güeá *f.*, güevada *f.*

submissive (man) *n.* jote *m.*

suburb *n.* localidad *f.*

sulk *v.* amurrarse
Sunday *n.* fomingo *m.*
superbly *adv.* descueve
supermarket *n.* super *m.*
supply *v.* aperarse
suspicious *n.* cachuo *m.*
swear-word *n.* garabato *m.*
sweatshirt *n.* polerón *m.*
sweetbread *n.* queque *m.*
sweetheart *n.* cachipurri *m.*, cosita *f.*
sweet-talk *v.* engrupir
swelling *n.* cototo *m.*
sycophant *n.* chupamedias *m.*
sycophantic *adj.* arrastrado

T

taciturn *adj.* taimao
take on *v.* lumear
talkative *adj.* chachero, toyento
tall (person) *n.* palote, girafa
tape (adhesive) *n.* huincha *f.*
tape (scotch) *n.* scotch *m.*
tasteless *adj.* fome, fomeque
television *n.* tevé *f.*
tempestuous *adj.* lunático
temporary work *n.* pituto *m.*
tender *adj.* tiernucho
ten-peso coin *n.* zota *f.*
ten thousand-peso bill *n.* arturo *m.*
terrific *adj.* bacán, choro, caballo, groso, güendy
test (in school) *n.* cátedra *f.*
thief *n.* lanza
thing *n.* guarifaifa *f.*, huifa *f.*, cuestión *f.*
thirst *n.* cecilia *f.*

thong *n.* colaless *m.*
timid *adj.* achunchado
tipsy *adj.* entonado
tired *adj.* chato, decaído, pajeado, cabreado
to *prep.* pal, pa'
to end *v.* chispotear, clotear
to get drugged *v.* volar
toilet paper *n.* confort *m.*
tons *adv.* caleta
toothless *adj.* cindy
touch *v.* agarrar
touchy *adj.* mañoso
tough *adj.* aliñado
traffic jam *n.* taco *m.*
traffic ticket *n.* parte *m.*
traffic warning *n.* educativo *m.*
traitor *n.* vaca, vacuna
tranquil *adj.* piola
travel *v.* patiperrear
travel-lover *n.* patiperro
trick *n.* pillería *f.*
trick *v.* embrollar
trifle *n.* maní *m.*
trip-up *n.* trancailla *f.*
triviality *n.* lesera *f.*
troubled *adj.* cagado
truant *n.* cimarra *f.*
truth *n.* posta *f.*, pulenta *f.*, dura *f.*
t-shirt *n.* polera *f.*
turtleneck *n.* beatle *m.*

U

ugly *adj.* feín, guata (woman)
unaccompanied *adj.* botella
unathletic *adj.* fofo

understand *v.* cachar
underwear *n.* (women's) *m.pl.* cuadros
uneducated *adj.* porro
unintelligent *adj.* perquinazo
unkempt *adj.* destartalado
unlikeable (person) *n.* perno *m.*, ladrillo *m.*
unlucky (person) *n.* yeta
unmotivated *adj.* funado
urine *n.* pichí *m.*
U.S.A. *n.* Gringolandia *f.*

V

vegetables (green) *n.* pasto *m.*
very *adv.* re
vexed *adj.* enrollado
V.I.P. *n.* veep *m.*
vomit *n.* guajardo *m.*
vulgar *adj.* chihua, peliento, roto, pulento, chana, picante, punga, torreja, pinganilla, piruja, cuma, flaite, guachaca

W

wait *v.* aguantar
wander *v.* patiperrear
warmth *n.* nanai *m.*
warning *n.* guarda *f.*
warrior *n.* chúcaro, warrier
watch *v.* lorear
water bottle *n.* guatero *m.*
water heater *n.* cálifont
water-lover *n.* pirigüin
weak *adj.* debilucho, ñegla
wealthy (person) *n.* paltón

well *adv.* flor
well-connected *adj.* apitutado
well-dressed *adj.* cacharpeado, emperifollao
whack *n.* chachazo *m.*
whipping *n.* guascazo *m.*
white (esp. face) *adj.* paliducho
wife *n.* eñora *f.*, pierna *f.*, bruja *f.*, peuca *f.*, mi peor es na
wine (mulled) *n.* navegado *m.*
wisecracker *n.* pelusa
witch doctor *n.* meico *m.*, machi (*m.*, *f.*)
woman *n.* reina *f.* zorra (*derog.*), yegua (*derog.*)
womanizer *n.* lacho, picarón, picaflor, pololo (all *m.*)
work *n.* pega *f.*
worsen *v.* chacrearse
wound *n.* yaya *f.*

Y

yes *adv.* ya, sifri
youth *n.* lolo, mino, moquillento (*derog.*)
yucky (*sl.*) *adj.* tóxico
yuppy *n./adj.* cuico

Anglicismos
(Adopted English Words)

Chileans adopt English words with a passion, sometimes using them intentionally, other times not even knowing that their words derive from English. Over time, Chileans have adapted some of these words to mean something somewhat different. The notes in parentheses explain the specific definition that Chileans use when that English word has several definitions or they provide some other clarification.

after hour (after-hours bar)
baby-sitter
background
bar
barman
behavior
best-seller
blazer (dress jacket)
boom (rapid growth)
boxer (only the singular is used; refers to boxer briefs)
break
bus
call center
candy
casting (try-out)
chance
chef (the word is also, of course, French)
clóset (note the accent on the o)
close-up

cool
copyright
diet
email
encounter (reunion, meeting)
express
fan (supporter)
feeling
freak
freezer
full
full-time
gay
go-go dancer
hacker
Halloween (this has been celebrated in Chile since
    the early 90s)
happy
happy hour
hippy
hit (the term "greatest hits" is also used)
hobby
in (inside)
insight
Internet
ketchup
light (used as an adjective; i.e., not heavy)
living (living room, sofa)
lobby (used as a noun; i.e., the entrance in a hotel)
loft (used as a noun; i.e., an apartment)
lollipop
look (used as a noun; used to mean an attractive
    appearance, the "look")
mall (shopping mall)
manager
marketing
metrosexual

nerd
night club
notebook (laptop computer)
out (outside)
partner
part-time
peak (as in peak hour)
performance
personal trainer
premiere (opening night)
pub
rack
rating
ring (boxing)
royalty (i.e., a share of proceeds)
sandwich
sex symbol
sexy
shopping (shopping mall)
short (short pants)
show
single (as in her first single from her new album)
spa
spot (advertisement)
spray
striptease
súper
taxi
team
thriller (used as an adjective: scary, frightening)
ticket
top (best)
topless
tour
zapping (with remote control)

Phrasebook

Greetings, Polite Expressions, and Small Talk

In Chile people greet each other warmly and often end up in long conversations about families and friends. When Chileans see old friends or meet new people they kiss them on both cheeks, or give firm embraces. In Chile when you see someone you know you are expected to stop and talk for a few minutes, even when in a hurry. Consequently, there are more than just a handful of polite expressions used to catch up with people or to break the ice.

Please note that Spanish punctuation calls for an upside-down exclamation point or question mark at the beginning of a phrase, as well as one at the end.

¿Cómo andamio?
How are things going?

¿Quiúbo?
What's up?

¿Qué talca?
What's up?

¿Qué onda?
What's going on?

¿Qué onda, microonda?
What's going on?

¿Qué se teje?
> What's going on?
> What is one sowing?

¿Cómo le vaca?
> How are you?
> How is the cow to you?

¿Cómo estadio?
> How are you?
> How is the stadium?

¿Cómo le baila?
> How are you?
> How does it dance for you?

¿Y bosnia?
> And you?

¿Y boston?
> And you?

¿Y albornoz?
> And you?

¿Y turra?
> And you?

¿Quién soy?
> Who are you?

¡Qué tienes?
> What's the matter?

¿Cachai?
You know? You understand?

¿Me entendí?
You know? Do you understand?

¿Qué cosa?
What?

¿Quién te metió ficha?
Who invited you into the conversation?

¿A cómo estamos hoy?
What day is it today?

¿Qué container?
What do you have to say?

¿Cuánto?
What is your last name?
Note: One asks this after hearing the person's
first name. Ex. ¿Juan cuánto? means What is
Juan's last name?

Ahí estoy.
I'm fine.

Aquí estamos.
I'm fine.

Estoy bien, pasándola.
I'm fine and carrying on.

Estoy al otro litro.
I'm fine/ok.

Están cayendo los patos asados.
It's very hot.

Hay vemos.
We'll see.

Nos belmont.
See you later.

Nos cachamos.
See you later.

Nos vidrios.
See you later.

Chavela.
Good-bye.

Porfa, porfís.
Please.

Graciela.
Thank you.

No hay por qué.
Don't mention it.

Te perdiste.
You haven't been around in a while.

¿Te fijas?
Do you understand? You see?
lit: Do you pay attention?

Que te vaya bonito.
> Have a nice day.

Te combina.
> It suits you.

Todo esta saliendo viento en popa.
> Everything's going well.

Exclamations

In Chile many people like to draw attention to themselves, either by screaming something at the top of their lungs or by unleashing a quick and biting turn of a phrase. Many a time you will find Chilean parents snapping at their children in order to keep them in line, as is typical in this society in which strict discipline reigns. Such outbursts have helped give rise to a slew of local exclamations, provided below.

¡Filo!
It doesn't matter! Forget about it!

¿A dónde la viste?
What are you talking about?!
lit: To where did you see it?!

¿Cómo se te ocurre?
What are you talking about?!

¡Dale!
Do it! Go ahead!

¡Déjate!
Cut it out! Stop it!

¡Miércale!
Ugh! Darn! [used as a form of surprise and dismay]

¡Chanta la moto!
Calm down! Stop it!
lit: Stop the motorcycle!

¡Chaucha!
Careful! Watch out!

¡Gánate acá!
Come here!

¡Ven paca!
Come here!

¡Anda palla!
Go over there!

¡Ya pues!
Come on! Let's go!

¡Pégate la ascurría!
Behave yourself!

¡Fuera!
Get out!

¡Olvídate!
Forget it!

¡Ni cagando!
No way!

¿Y qué tiene?
So what?

¡Hasta cuándo la revuelves!
Stop screwing around!

Exclamations

¡La jodió!
He/she was screwed!

¡De miedo!
Fantastic!
lit: Of fear!

¡Matan!
They're fantastic!
lit: They kill!

¡Mira tú!
Wow! Impressive!

¡Mortal!
Terrific!
lit: Deadly

¡Bacán!
Cool!

¡Güeno!
Great! [emphatic form of "¡Bueno!"]

¡De película!
Fantastic!
lit: From a movie!

¡Bien bueno!
Excellent!

¡Chuata!
Darn! Shucks!

¡Recórcholis!
Darn! Shucks!

¡Chanfles!
Darn! Shucks!

¡Conchalevale!
Darn! Shucks!

¡Pucha, la cuestión!
That's awful!

¡Pucha!
Damn!

¡Má malo!
The absolute worse!

¡Viste!
You see!

¡Súbete a la micro!
Tune in to what's going on!
lit: Get on the bus!

¡Hazme caso!
Obey me! Listen to me!

Money

The Chilean monetary unit is the peso. There are 1-peso, 5-peso, 10-peso, 50-peso, 100-peso, and 500-peso coins. Bills are available in denominations of 500, 1,000, 5,000, 10,000, and 20,000 pesos.

Basic Monetary Terms

¿Cuánto vale?
How much is it?

¿Cuánto sale?
How much is it?

billullo (*n.m.*)
money

chaucha (*n.f.*)
money

plata (*n.f.*)
money

molido (*n.m.*)
loose change
lit: ground up

turro (*n.m.*)
stack (esp. of bills)

choro (*n.m.*)
    change purse

vaca (*n.f.*)
    money pooled together
    lit: a cow

hacer una polla
    to collect money
    lit: to make a chicken

vale (*n.m.*)
    receipt

Denominations

zota (*n.f.*)
    10-peso coin

gamba (*n.f.*)
    100 pesos
    lit: a prawn

quina (*n.f.*)
    500 pesos

luca (*n.f.*)
    1,000-peso bill

lucrecia (*n.f.*)
    1,000-peso bill

gabriela (*n.f.*)
    5,000-peso bill

arturo (*n.m.*)
10,000-peso bill

palo (*n.m.*)
1 million pesos
lit: a stick

guaton (*n.m.*)
1 million pesos

Phrases

¿Cuándo canta Gardel?
When do they pay wages?

pagar el piso
to invite everyone out on your tab after you get
your first paycheck
lit: to pay the floor

vale hongo
it's worthless
lit: it's worth a mushroom

vale callampa
it's worthless
lit: it's worth a mushroom

no salva a nadie
he/she is worthless
lit: he/she doesn't save anyone

andar dulce
to go out with money (on you)
lit: to walk around sweet

---

andar con el menso mazo
>to go out with a lot of money (on you)

andar seco
>to go out without money (on you)
>lit: to walk around dry

tener más plata que pelo en la cabeza
>to be rich
>lit: to have more money than hair on the head

cargado (*adj.*)
>full of money
>lit: loaded, charged

andar pato
>to walk around without money
>lit: to walk as a duck

pato, calato, cinco (*adj.*)
>broke, penniless
>lit: duck

estar cagado del mate
>to be chintzy

pistolero de lo bueno
>refers to someone who is chintzy (cheap)

botado (*adj.*)
>cheap, inexpensive

andar a la bolsa
>to be a mooch

bolsero (*n./adj.*)
mooch

cachurero (*n.*)
someone who saves everything

cafiche (*n.*)
exploiter, pimp, someone using another for
their money

Food and Dining

Chilean food includes a fantastic mix of salsas, stews, casseroles, fish dishes, and much, much more. And while Chilean wine has been catching on for years in the U.S., back at home it has long been sacred. The meal as both a dining and social occasion is very important in Chile, as it is a time when family members and friends come together and show their love and warmth for one another.

Basic Terms

papeo (*n.m.*)
  food

chatarra (*n.f.*)
  junk food, fast food
  lit: scrap iron

fritanga (*n.f.*)
  fried food

once (*n.f.*)
  light, evening meal, tea
  lit: eleven

mangi (*n.m.*)
  meal

menú (*n.m.*)
  prix-fixe meal (fixed-price meal)

casino (*n.m.*)
  cafeteria
  lit: casino

tenedor libre
  all-you-can-eat buffet
  lit: free fork

picada (*n.f.*)
  inexpensive restaurant
  lit: a sting

súper (*n.m.*)
  supermarket
  lit: super

manyar (*v.*)
  to eat

agarraguire (*n.*)
  glutton

gasuso (*adj.*)
  hungry

languí (*adj.*)
  hungry

cecilia (*n.f.*)
  thirst

Phrases

tomar once
>to have the late afternoon (or early evening) meal
>lit: to take eleven

¡Al rancho!
>Let's eat!
>lit: To the ranch!

¡A manyar!
>Let's eat!

¡A papear!
>Let's eat!

te viene siguiendo el léon
>you're very hungry
>lit: the lion is following you

te crujen las tripas
>you're very hungry
>lit: your intestine is crackling

andar con el diente largo
>to be very hungry
>lit: to walk around with a long tooth

probar tu mano
>to try your food
>lit: to try your hand

tener buena mano
>to cook well
>lit: to have a good hand

a la suerte de la olla

    to arrive at someone's house not knowing what food they will be offering

    lit: to the luck of the pot

tener una guata de pajarito

    to have a tiny stomach, describes someone not inclined to eat

    lit: to have a bird's stomach

tener una guata de cachureos

    to have an iron stomach

comer como condenado

    to eat an extraordinary amount

    lit: to eat like a condemned person

tener cecilia

    to be thirsty

estar seco

    to be thirsty

    lit: to be dry

estar más seco que un escupo de momia

    to be very thirsty

    lit: to be dryer than a mummy's spit

tener más sed que piojo de muñeca

    to be very thirsty

    lit: to be thirstier than a louse on a doll

tener más sed que toalla hippy

    to be very thirsty

    lit: to be thirstier than the towel of a hippy

disculpe lo poco
> sorry for the lack of food (often said
> sarcastically)

Guatita llena, corazón contento
> A full stomach makes for a content heart

para chuparse los dedos
> finger lickin' good
> lit: for sucking the fingers

ropa vieja
> leftovers
> lit: old clothes

pájaro que comió, voló
> refers to someone who eats and runs
> lit: the bird that ate flew away

Comida hecha, amistad deshecha
> When the meal's done, the friendship's done
> (said jocularly)
> lit: Food done, friendship undone

Foods and Drinks

choca, coquita (*n.f.*)
> tea

mate (*n.m.*)
> dried herbal tea

bebida (*n.f.*)
> soda, soft drink

chela, chelita (*n.f.*)
  beer

caña (*n.f.*)
  small cup of wine

jote (*n.m.*)
  drink of Coke and red wine

chupilca (*n.f.*)
  alcoholic cider with toasted flour

combinado (*n.m.*)
  mixture of Pisco brandy and a type of soft drink
      (esp. Coke or Sprite)
  lit: combined

navegado (*n.m.*)
  warm wine with orange peel and spices
  lit: traveled (adj.)

chambreado (*adj.*)
  warm—usually refers to heated wine

tintano (*n.m.*)
  red wine

tintero (*n.*)
  red wine-lover

durazno (*n.m.*)
  peach

frutilla (*n.f.*)
  strawberry

limón de pica (*n.m.*)
  lime

palta (*n.f.*)
  avocado

penca (*n.f.*)
  green vegetable like celery

zapallo (*n.m.*)
  calabaza (so-named in U.S. Latin stores)

pila (*n.f.*)
  bunch of fruit or vegetables

doblada (*n.f.*)
  bread folded in layers

hallulla (*n.f.*)
  thick English muffin-type bread

lulo (*n.m.*)
  long flat bread

marraqueta (*n.f.*)
  French bread

pan amasado
  homemade bread

queque (*n.m.*)
  sweet bread

sopaipilla (*n.f.*)
  fried bread fritter

anticucho (*n.m.*)
  shish kebab

asado (*n.m.*)
  barbecue

prieta (*n.f.*)
blood sausage

tuto, trutro (*n.m.*)
chicken thigh

choro, chorito, cholga (*n.m.*)
mussel

jaiva (*n.f.*)
crab

ají (*n.m.*)
chile pepper

merquén (*n.m.*)
ground hot red pepper

pebre (*n.m.*)
salsa, hot sauce

cazuela (*n.f.*)
stew, hearty meat soup

pantruca (*n.f.*)
white dough soup

pilco (*n.m.*)
corn kernels

quaker (*n.m.*)
oatmeal

maní (*n.m.*)
peanut

poroto (*n.m.*)
bean

cabritas *(n.f.pl.)*
  popcorn

pan *(n.m.)*
  a stick of butter

fondo *(n.m.)*
  large pot (for cooking in the countryside)

chancaca *(n.f.)*
  solid brown sugar

manjar *(n.m.)*
  caramel cream (also known as dulce de leche)
  lit: delicacy, food

jalea *(n.f.)*
  Jell-O
  lit: jelly

royal *(n.m.)*
  baking powder

Kitchen Equipment

un, dos, tres
  food processor

uslero *(n.m.)*
  rolling pin

hervir la pava
  to boil water in a tea kettle
  lit: to boil the turkey

The Body and Clothes

Chileans can be divided into two types: those that obsess over their bodies and clothes and those that simply let it all go. The former watch what they eat closely, pump up or trim down in the gym, go heavy on the makeup and hair dye, and choose the most modern of fashions. Attire with a conservative air usually triumphs. In contrast, much of the rest of society comes across (at least to Americans) as grungy or free-spirited. Men let facial hair run rampant or have ponytails, and dark, baggy clothes are commonplace.

Parts of the Body

callampa *f.*
bowl-shaped haircut

caluga *f.*
stomach muscle

champa *f.*
bushy hair, big head of hair

chocho *m.*
curl of hair

cogote *m.*
neck

gaña *f.*
  sand in the eyes from sleeping

guata *f.*
  belly, stomach

hocico *m.*, *f.*
  big mouth

luceros *m.pl.*
  beautiful eyes

moño *m.*
  ponytail

narigón
  big nose

narizazo *m.*
  big nose

ojudo
  big eyes

paila *f.*
  large ear

patas de gallo *f.pl.*
  crow's feet

ponchera *f.*, **talaje** *m.*, **tambembe** *m.*
  beer belly

poto *m.*, **queque** *m.*, **cola** *f.*, **cachete** *m.*
  buttocks

pulpo *m.*
bellybutton

rollo *m.*
roll of fat

sobaco *m.*
armpit

tarro *m.*
mouth

visagra *f.*
knee

zapallo *m.*
head

Clothes

bachata *f.*, **chalupa** *f.*
house slippers

beatle *m.*
turtleneck

bluyines *m.pl.*, **pecosbiles** *m.pl.*
blue jeans

chalina *f.*
scarf

chupalla *f.*
hat

chiteco *m.*
cloth

cuadros *m.pl.*
underwear (women's)

guasca *f.*
belt, strap

jockey *m.*
cap, baseball hat

pantis *f.pl.*
panty hose, stockings

papa *f.*
hole in clothes

persa *n.f.*
market where used or old products (including
clothes) are sold

pilchas *f.pl.*
clothes

polera *f.*
t-shirt

polerón *m.*
sweatshirt

soquete *m.*
short sock

Holidays

While Chileans are known to work among the longest hours in the world, they also benefit from an indulgent schedule of holidays. These include special days for policemen, children, and a legion of saints. Chileans love to make "sandwiches" too. For example, when Thursday is an official day off, they take off Friday too, which is the filler day (the "sandwich meat" perhaps?) between Thursday and Saturday (serving as the "bread" for the sandwich). Holidays are a time when many families leave big cities such as Santiago and head to the beautiful coast or spectacular mountains.

Día de los Carabineros
  Policemen's Day

Día del Niño
  Children's Day

Glorias Navales
  Commemorates Chile's defeat to Peru in the Battle of Iquique (May 21)

Día de los Muertos
  Day of the Dead

Halloween
  Halloween

dulce o travesura
　　trick-or-treat at Halloween
　　lit: sweet or prank

Fiestas Patrias
　　Independence Day celebrations (September 18
　　　　and 19)

cueca (*n.f.*)
　　Chile's national dance; danced primarily during
　　　　the weekend of *Fiestas Patrias*.

Pascua (*n.f.*)
　　Christmas

Pascua de Los Conejos
　　Easter

Pascua de Resurrección
　　Easter

Viejo Pascuero
　　Santa Claus

dieciocho chico
　　A weeklong celebration starting on the Monday
　　　　following the week of the September 18
　　　　(Independence Day) celebration.

hacer sandwich
　　to take an extra day as holiday because it falls
　　　　between two days off
　　lit: to make a sandwich

Distance, Time, and Travel

"¡Tantas lunas!" said my friend when we saw each other for the first time in many months. This would occasion many to look up at the sky and count the moons. But my quizzical look said enough, and he quickly told me that it had simply been so long since we had seen each other. It reminded me that in Chile—where people are often late and do not eyeball their watches—time can sometimes be better measured in moons than in minutes or days.

Periods of Time

una vez a las mil
     once in a blue moon, very seldom
     lit: one time in a thousand

uno en un millón
     once in a blue moon, very seldom
     lit: one time in a million

el año de la pera
     eons ago
     lit: the year of the pear

el año de la coco
     eons ago
     lit: the year of the coconut

el año del pico
> eons ago
> lit: the year of the beak

estar más viejo que la biblia
> to be extremely old
> lit: to be older than the bible

¡Tantas lunas!
> It's been so long!
> lit: So many moons!

un dos por tres
> in a moment, soon

altiro (*adv.*)
> immediately

en tres tiempos
> very quickly

ir hecho un peo
> to leave in a big hurry

hacerla cortita
> to do it very rapidly

de ahí
> later

al toque
> shortly

de un día para otro
> overnight

un medio pique
> a long journey

día por medio
> every other day

a lo lejos
> from time to time

Phrases

ir pegando
> to leave on the dot, to leave at a precise time

salir pegando
> to leave immediately, to leave at that very
> moment
> lit: to go glueing

echarse el pollo
> to get out of town, leave
> lit: to throw out the chicken

los juimos
> we left, we went away

calabaza, calabaza, cada uno pa' su casa
> let's each go home
> lit: pumpkin, pumpkin, each one for his home

poner la piñénienta
> to floor it (in a car), to accelerate rapidly

meter la chala
> to floor it (in a car)

Modes of Transportation

hacer dedo
  to hitchhike
  lit: to do the finger

cleta (*n.f.*)
  bike

papú (*n.m.*)
  car

cacharro (*n.m.*)
  old car

movíl (*n.m.*)
  radio taxi

micro (*n.m.*)
  local bus

pan de molde (*n.m.*)
  freight train

Going Out, Cigarettes, and Booze

Chileans love to go out and party. Wine and beer are the most popular drinks, along with the country's favorite cocktail, Pisco Sour. Even on weekdays people often go out until late, and on weekends it's not unusual for youths to start their evenings at 11 PM and finally wind their way home at 5 or 6 AM. If you join in, expect to wash your clothes the next day: smoking is a national pastime.

Phrases

tirar la chirola
to dress well, look nice

echarse una manito de gato
to put on makeup
lit: to throw in the little hand (paw) of a cat

afirmarse el clima
to arrange oneself, tidy up, get dressed up
lit: to steady the climate

carretear (*v.*)
to go out and party

carrete (*n.m.*)
partying, evening night out

carretero (*n.*)
a party animal

seguir la cueca
to continue the party

pasarlo a la pinta
to have a great time

pasarlo regio
to have a great time

pasarlo chancho
to have a great time
lit: to spend it pig

chori (*adj.*)
entertaining, fun

las buenas, las malas
the good times, the bad times

Smoking

pucho (*n.m.*)
cigarette

carretonero (*n.*)
heavy smoker

chimenea (*n.*)
heavy smoker
lit: chimney

fumar como carretonera
to smoke heavily

fumar más que una chimenea
    to smoke heavily
    lit: to smoke more than a chimney

fumar como camello
    to smoke heavily
    lit: to smoke like a camel

Drinking

copete (*n.m.*)
    alcoholic drink

municiones (*n.f.pl.*)
    mixed drinks
    lit: munitions

curarse (*v.refl.*)
    to get drunk
    lit: to cure oneself

estar arriba de la pelota
    to be drunk
    lit: to be on top of the ball

entrar agua al bote
    to be drunk
    lit: to enter water into the boat

apagar la tele
    to lose consciousness due to excess alcohol
    lit: to turn off the television

se calienta la jeta
    I want to keep drinking
    lit: the snout's getting hot

se calienta el hocico
> I want to keep drinking
> lit: the snout's getting hot

chupar como una esponja
> to drink heavily
> lit: to suck like a sponge

¡Al seco!
> Bottom's up!

¡Catorce!
> Bottom's up!
> lit: Fourteen!

chupai más que orilla de playa
> you're a heavy drinker
> lit: you suck in more than the seashore

Relationships: Love and Intrigue

Soap operas are revered in Chile, and relationships in the country are so rife with love and intrigue that truth is often stranger than fiction. Infidelity is hardly uncommon and often serves as the talk of the day. While historically men have been known as "players," some argue that the macho culture is eroding and with greater women's rights comes less betrayal. The culture is also changing in other ways: in the new millennium divorce is no longer illegal in Chile.

Roles in Relationships

pololo (*n.m.*)
  boyfriend; womanizer

polola (*n.f.*)
  girlfriend

novio (*n.m.*)
  fiancé

novia (*n.f.*)
  fiancé

amigo (–a) con ventaja
  refers to habitual, consensual sex between
    friends
  lit: friend with advantage

cachipurri (*n.m.*)
sweetheart

cosita (*n.f.*)
dear, sweetheart

peuca (*n.f.*)
wife, girlfriend

pierna (*n.f.*)
wife, girlfriend
lit: leg

bruja (*n.f.*)
wife
lit: witch

pata negra
the lover of a woman
lit: black foot (paw)

picao a la araña
a man who likes to seduce women

chicha fresca
a woman-chaser

profanador de cunas
a cradle-robber (*sl.*), one who looks for a
relationship with someone much younger
than they
lit: a defiler of cribs

buen partido
a previously eligible bachelor, a good catch
lit: a good game/match

media naranja
> ideal person or mate
> lit: half orange (or "huge orange" in Chile,
>   since media refers to size)

conpinche
> lover

uña y mugre
> very close friends
> lit: fingernail and dirt

The Conquest

piñiscar la uva
> to seduce a woman who's already taken

arrastrarse (*v.refl.*)
> to try to win over someone uninterested in you
> lit: to crawl

tirarse al dulce
> to aggressively try to conquer a woman
> lit: to throw yourself to the sweet

estar más entrado
> to be bold and aggressive in trying to conquer
>   someone (amorously)

pasarse para la punta
> to hit on someone rudely

pasar de la raya
> to go over the line

pasar de listo
> to be out of bounds, to be out of line (*sl.*)

puntudo (*adj.*)
>   out of bounds with a woman, hitting on
>   someone rudely

Dating

te voy a hacer el gancho con mi amiga
>   I'll set you up (on a date) with my friend

andar (con alguien)
>   to date casually

pinchar (*v.*)
>   to hook up with (amorously), to have a fling
>   with

tirar (*v.*)
>   to hook up with (amorously), to have a fling
>   with
>   lit: to throw

pololear (*v.*)
>   to date (as "official" boyfriend-girlfriend)

quedarse con los crespos hechos
>   to be left with great desire (e.g., by a woman
>   you wanted to conquer, who perhaps stood
>   you up)
>   lit: to remain with curls done

tocar el violín
>   to be a third wheel (*idm.*), refers to the person
>   who uncomfortably accompanies an
>   amorous couple
>   lit: to play the violin

Relationships: Love and Intrigue

A rey muerto, rey puesto
you lost one mate, but found another

¡Mijita rica!
What a babe!

¡Mijito rico!
What a hunk!

cocoroco (*adj.*)
flirtatious

atracar (*v.*)
to kiss

pato (*n.m.*)
a kiss

calugazo (*n.m.*)
a smooch

¡No comaí delante de los pobres!
Don't smooch in front of us!
lit: Don't eat in front of the poor!

¡No contar la plata delante de los pobres!
Don't smooch in front of us!
lit: Don't count your money in front of the
poor!

estar enamorado hasta las patas
to be head over heels over, to be madly in love
lit: to be in love down to the feet (paws)

parecen unos canarios
they're like lovebirds

Marriage

casarse de blanco
>   to get married as a virgin
>   lit: to get married in white

ir a uscar a la iñora
>   to go look for one's wife

andar con la pierna
>   to go out with one's wife or girlfriend
>   lit: to go out with the leg

apiernado (*adj.*)
>   refers to a man who's out with his wife or
>   girlfriend

Betrayal

pegar en la nuca
>   to cheat on someone
>   lit: to hit in the nape

poner el gorro
>   to cheat on someone
>   lit: to put on the cap

poner los cuernos
>   to cheat on someone
>   lit: to put on the horns

jugar chueco
>   to cheat on someone
>   lit: to play crooked

subirse por el chorro
> to cheat on someone
> lit: to go up towards the stream

dorar la píldora
> to cheat on someone
> lit: to glaze the pill

gorrear
> to cheat on someone

cagar
> to cheat on someone
> lit: to soil

gorrero (*n.*)
> someone who cheats on their significant other

pico en el ojo
> a betrayal
> lit: a beak in the eye

quedó la escoba
> it unleashed a scandal
> lit: the broom fell

sacar pica
> to make someone jealous
> lit: to take out a lance

Breaking Up

o te tiras o mejor te quedas
> either you stay or go

cortar por lo sano
> to end (esp. a relationship)
> lit: to cut it by the sane (way)

dar filo
> to end a relationship
> lit: to give a sharp edge

mandar cortado
> to abandon, leave, reject, throw out

dar vuelta a la página
> to move on
> lit: to turn the page

Friendship

caerse bien con
> to get along with

estar en mala con alguien
> to be at war with someone

tener mal a alguien
> to not like someone

yo no lo paso/yo no la paso
> I don't get along with him/her

Intelligence and Ignorance

As an American in a foreign place, you can feel a bit like a fool at first. That is certainly the case in Chile, where you may not be familiar with the customs or the local language—yes, Chilenismos. There are innumerable expressions to indicate that someone is a numskull in Chile. The terms, however, are not harsh, but rather playful so take them with a grain of salt. And when you get settled and start picking up Chilenismos, you will hear someone call you *capo*, (see below) and you'll feel a whole lot better.

Intelligence

te crugió el mate
> you thought of something intelligent

tener dedos para el piano
> to have talent
> lit: to have fingers for the piano

tener ni un pelo de tonto
> to be not at all stupid
> lit: to have not even a hair of foolishness

cabezón (*n.*)
> an intelligent person
> lit: a big head

capo (*adj.*), **caperuzo** (*adj.*)
    intelligent

aguja (*adj.*)
    quick-witted

un zero a la izquierda
    someone inept at something
    lit: a zero to the left

tener el pan hecho
    to have already done what someone is asking, to
        be one step ahead (*idm.*)
    lit: to have the bread made

Ignorance

no le pega a la/el . . .
    he doesn't understand . . .

no le achunta a la/el . . .
    he doesn't understand . . .

te están cantando y no bailai
    you don't understand
    lit: they're singing to you and you don't dance

tener una cabeza de pollo
    to be brainless, have an empty head
    lit: to have a chicken's head

tener una cabeza de cuesco
    to be brainless, have an empty head
    lit: to have a head of stone

no entender ni a palo
> to understand absolutely nothing about what is
> being explained

mata de huevas
> imbecile

se me fue
> I forgot

la risa abunda en la boca de los tontos
> you are a fool to laugh (said when one is telling
> someone something serious and they start
> laughing for no reason at all)
> lit: laughter abounds in the mouth of fools

Sloth and Indifference

It's easy to get in a lazy kind of mood in Chile—especially during the summer. It almost never rains and the beaches are packed from the northern coast of Iquique to Chiloé in the south. When I lie at Viña del Mar with the sun's rays scorching down, in no time *me quedo lona*. That is, suddenly I am sprawled on the beach unconscious, like a boxer on the canvas after receiving a stiff uppercut (which gives rise to the Chilean expression).

Sloth

cortar la leche
    to tire, make lazy
    lit: to cut the milk

dar paja
    to make lazy
    lit: to give straw

tirarse las huevas
    to be lazy, do nothing
    lit: to throw out the row

machucar el membrillo
    to be lazy, do nothing
    lit: to crush the quince

un poto blando
a couch potato

hacer tuto
to sleep

tirarse un ratito
to take a nap

irse a la lona
to fall deeply asleep, be out like a light (*idm.*)
lit: to go to the canvas

quedarse lona
to plunge into a deep sleep, to pass out (*idm.*)
Note. This differs from the above term because
quedarse lona is to fall asleep accidentally,
whereas *irse a la lona* is intentional.

estar hecho bolsa
to be totally beat

dar la cacha
to waste one's time

parar el dedo
to waste one's time
lit: to stop the finger

sacar la vuelta
to waste one's time

fofo, pajero, pánfilo, porro (*adj.*)
lazy

Indifference

no me pesca
> it doesn't interest me
> lit: it doesn't fish me

se me echó la yegua
> I lost interest

no estar ni ahí
> it doesn't matter to me

me da lo mismo
> I couldn't care less; Whatever, it's the same
> to me

me da igual
> It's all the same to me; I don't care

me importa un pico
> I don't give a damn

¿Y qué tanto?
> And what does it matter? And who cares?

(hacer algo) al peo
> (to do something) without thought or effort,
> haphazardly

Effort and Work

Despite Chile's stunning economic growth in past decades, at least in Latin American terms, it can be pretty tough to make a buck in the country. More than a few times I listened as people told me how they had to *sacarse la mugre* or "work their fanny off" just to put food on the table. As is often the case in Chile, many different expressions evolved for this very common sentiment in order to give more variety and life to the local language.

Effort

a todo morrison/morri
    at full blast, no holes-barred

a todo dar
    at full blast, no holes-barred

a todo cachete
    at full speed

poner chala
    to increase speed

poner las pilas
    to give it your all
    lit: to put in batteries

---

poner talento
>   to give it your all
>   lit: to put talent

ponerle bueno
>   to give it your all

ponerle güendy
>   to give it your all

ponerle pechito
>   to give it your all

ponerle pino
>   to give it your all

ponerle color
>   to give it your all

a concho
>   completely, full, to the maximum, at full blast

irse al chancho
>   to go to the extreme; to overdo it
>   lit: to go to the pig

hasta la baba
>   until the last drop, or until the last bit
>   lit: until the spittle

hasta el concho
>   until the last drop, or until the last bit

hasta las patas
>   to the maximum
>   lit: until the feet/paws

pega (*n.f.*)
work

sacarse la mugre
to work one's rear off
lit: to remove the dirt from oneself

sacarse la cresta
to work one's rear off
lit: to remove the crest from oneself

trabajar como chino
to work around the clock
lit: to work like a Chinese person

trabajar por bolitas de dulce
to work for almost nothing
lit: to work for sweet little balls

pagar el piso
to take out all your friends by paying with the
first paycheck of your new job
lit: to pay for the floor

el pan de cada día
the routine
lit: everyday bread

Personality Traits and Types of People

Sickly

estar pa' la corneta
   to be sick or exhausted

hacer mal
   to make sick

estar pa' la canta
   to be back, be sick

estar pa' la corneta
   to be sick or exhausted

estar pal gato
   to be bad, to be sick

está cagaí/cagado
   to be in bad shape (economically, emotionally, etc.)

(tener) cara de poto
   to appear sick, tired or pale

como las pelotas
   in bad shape
   lit: like balls

pate laucha
   weak-kneed, lacking in strength

pate lana
    weak-kneed, lacking in strength

le faltan palos p'al puente
    to be mentally ill
    lit: sticks are missing for the bridge

no le entran balas
    that person is in good health
    lit: bullets don't enter him/her

estar como palta
    to be bruised
    lit: to be like avocado

se te arranca la moto
    you're crazy
    lit: the motorcycle's pulling out from you

pela cables
    someone with bizarre thoughts

un bicho raro
    a weirdo
    lit: a rare bug

tirado de las mechas
    unrealistic, crazy
    lit: thrown from the wick

pasar rollos
    to imagine things that don't exist
    lit: to pass rolls

Eso es tirado de las mechas
    That is absurd

Surly

andar de maleta
to be riled up

estar hasta la coronilla
to be fed up

hincharse la vena
to get angry
lit: to have your vein swell

ponerse choro
to get angry

echar el mundo abajo
to blow up with anger
lit: to throw the world below

irse en picada
to go ballistic

pintar el mono (a alguien)
to blow up at someone (*ella me pintó el mono*
means she blew up at me)

andar con la lesera
to be ill-humored, angry

andar atrevasado
to go around with anger, fury

andar con los monos
to go around angry
lit: to go around with monkeys

apestarse (*v. refl.*)
> to become fed up with

despertarse/levantarse con la pata izquierda
> to wake up on the wrong side of the bed (*idm.*)
> lit: to wake up with the left foot (paw)

echar la foca
> to give a dirty look, threaten
> lit: to give the seal

sacar los choros del canasto
> to infuriate someone

¿Qué te saca de las casillas?
> What gets you really angry?

buscar la quinta pata al gato
> look for the last recourse, or look for
>> something that will anger the other person
>> ("get their goat")
> lit: to look for the cat's fifth leg

¿Por qué me tiras al choque?
> Why are you pushing me into it?
> lit: Why do you throw me into the crash?

No me friegue la cachimba.
> Don't bother me.

Ill-tempered, Obnoxious, Disagreeable

chupete de fierro
> lit: an iron pacifier

collar de sandía
  lit: a watermelon necklace

levantao de raja/levantado raja
  lit:

medio genio
  lit:

patas/pie de plomo
  lit: lead paws (feet)

saco de plomo
  lit: a bag of lead

soldadito de plomo
  lit: a little soldier of lead

mala leche
  lit: bad milk

mala onda
  lit: bad wave

cabro chico
  obnoxious, a little spoiled brat
  lit: a little goat

Proud

se quiebra
  he becomes very arrogant

creerse la muerte
  to be stuck-up
  lit: to believe you're death personified

Greedy

te gusta la ley del embudo
> you're selfish; you don't care about giving but
> rather only receiving
> lit: you like the law of the funnel

te gusta la del burro cachero
> all that matters is if it suits you; you always
> come first

mano de guagua
> stingy
> lit: the hand of a baby

piojo resucitado
> a poor person who became wealthy, snobby and
> classist
> lit: a resuscitated louse

cuico (*n./adj.*)
> yuppy; wealthy and arrogant person

jaibón (*n.*)
> a noble; person of wealth

Shameless

sin vergüenza (*n./adj.*)
> scoundrel; shameless
> lit: a without shame

care raja
> a shameless person

carepalo/care de palo (*n.m./adv.*)
a shameless person; bluntly, directly

alguien pasado pa la punta
someone disrespectful, presumptuous

Old

viejas teclas
elderly women
lit: old keys

viejo del saco
an imaginary man who takes children away
from their homes
lit: the old man of the bag

viejo sapo
a prying and curious old man
lit: an old frog

viejo verde
a dirty old man
lit: an old green man

Vulgar

pelagato (*n.m.*)
a coarse or vulgar person, poor guy, nobody

un ratón de acequia
a coarse individual

A Nobody

un peor es nada
   a nobody
   lit: a worse is nothing

usted no es na', ni chicha ni limoná'
   you're nobody, you are no one of importance
   lit: you are nothing—not cider, nor lemonade

poco hombre
   wimpy
   lit: little man

no tener pantalones
   to be a wimp, unmanly
   lit: to not have pants

estar arriba del columpio
   to be mocked
   lit: to be on the swing

chuparse entero
   to embarrass oneself
   lit: to suck oneself up whole

caerse la cara
   to embarrass oneself
   lit: to have one's face fall

¡Qué plancha!
   What an embarrassment!
   lit: What an iron!

Nervous

tener piulle en el poto
  to be jittery, uneasy or nervous

agachar el moño
  it makes me nervous

Types of Behavior

In Chilenismos the duck is not a mere animal, but serves as the core of many everyday expressions. For example *un pato* can be a kiss instead of a duck, and when roast ducks are falling from the sky (*están cayendo los patos asados*), it is very hot outside. Below there are additional expressions that use the waddler to make a point. For example, if I make little ducks (*hacer patitos*) then I am skipping a stone on water. And if I pay the duck (*pagar el pato*), I am bearing the brunt of something.

echar el poto a las moras
   to regret, recant

tirar el poto pa las moras
   to regret

tirar pa colina/pa la cola
   to regret

meter mano
   to mess with
   lit: to put in (a) hand

mandarse un condorito
   to ruin something

parar los carros
>to criticize; to draw attention
>lit: to stop the carts

tirar flores
>to compliment someone, say nice things about
>   someone
>lit: to throw flowers

hacer o hacerle caso
>to obey

tomar caldo de cabeza
>to be preoccupied with something
>lit: to have (take) head broth

dar el cuero
>to get psyched up
>lit: to give the leather

hacer patitos
>to skip a stone over the surface of water
>lit: to make little ducks

pagar el pato
>to pay the price, bear the brunt
>lit: to pay the duck

echar una mano
>to do a favor for someone
>lit: to throw a hand in

hacerse el lindo
>to act cute

Types of Behavior

estar caro pa' sacristán
  to act like you're impressive, when you're really not

me da cosas
  it makes me uneasy, uncomfortable
  lit: it gives me things

dar boleto
  to pay attention to

dar pelota
  to pay attention to
  lit: to give (a) ball

dar bolas
  to interest, to pay attention to
  lit: to give balls

ojo al charqui
  pay attention, beware
  lit: eye to (beware of) the beef jerky

andar aperrado
  to do whatever anyone demands

tomar papa
  to nurse (i.e., a baby on its mother's breast)

hacer la cimarra
  to play hookey

salir hasta en la sopa
  to repeatedly bump into someone or something
  lit: to go out even in the soup

cortar las huinchas
    to throw in the towel (*idm.*), give up

hablar hasta por los codos
    to chatter away, natter on
    lit: to speak even by way of the elbows

estar con el poto agarrado de las dos manos
    to be terrified

echar un luki
    to take a look

estar cagado de la risa
    to die laughing

sacarse el pillo
    to rationalize, justify something

andar a lo gringo
    to go around without wearing underwear

andar en paños menores
    to walk around in underwear

andar en pelota o en pelotillehue
    to be nude

pasarse la mano
    to go overboard

tener papas en la boca
    to speak in a stuffy or incomprehensible
        manner
    lit: to have potatoes in the mouth

hacer la pata
> to be nice to someone in order to get something
>> in return from them
> lit: to do the paw

levantar el pelo
> to improve, to boost the class or quality of
> lit: to lift the hair

anda a catear
> go and take a look
> to put your tail between your legs, to recognize
>> that you erred

tirarse a la piscina
> to wing it; to try to do something without having
>> the requisite experience, knowledge, etc.
> lit: to throw yourself into the pool

The Good and the Bad

One of the oddest aspects of Chilenismos is how they stray from Spanish grammatical rules. For example, rather than saying to someone "tú eres una buena persona" (you're a good person), they say "tú eres buena gente" (you're good people). If a Chilean tells you the latter while you're alone, don't think they are loopy or seeing double. It's just another Chilenismo and a high compliment indeed.

Goodness and Hospitality

ser buena gente
    to be a good person
    lit: to be good people (Note the singular
        Chilean translation)

tratar a alguien como la gente
    to treat someone well
    lit: to treat someone like the people

a la buena
    in a friendly manner

buena onda
    cool (*sl.*), hip, friendly
    lit: good wave

buena leche
   someone kind, friendly
   lit: good milk

buena tela
   a cool person
   lit: good cloth

ser más bueno que el pan
   to be a very kind person; innocent person
   lit: to be better than bread

ser un plato
   to be entertaining, to be fun
   lit: to be a plate

tener ángel
   to have a spark/to have a special allure
   lit: to have (an) angel

Evil and Inhospitable

ser mala gente
   to be a bad person
   lit: to be bad people (Note the singular Chilean
      translation)

que te vaya como el hoyo
   I hope it goes badly for you
   lit: I hope it goes like a hole for you

como el poto
   badly, horribly

hacer un mal
>to put a hex on
>lit: to do a bad

salir el tiro por la culata
>to go badly
>lit: for the shot to go out the butt of the revolver

estar como el forro
>to be terrible, unlikeable
>lit: to be like lining

ser pata de vaca
>to be cruel or bad with someone else
>lit: to be a cow's hoof (foot)

pegar en la pera
>to exploit someone
>lit: to hit in the chin (or "pear")

sacar el jugo
>to exploit
>lit: to withdraw the juice

no hay mal que por bien no venga
>among the bad there is something good

Truth and Lies

In Chile, the truth is sometimes hard to come by. Society encourages politeness and discourages confrontation, which makes people phrase their words gently, or just flat out lie. The proliferation of untruths—although many of them are merely white lies—has engendered a culture in which suspicion and distrust are abundant, as both Chileans and foreigners alike will attest. A premium is put on honest people who are true to their word.

Truth

cuando el río suena es porque piedras trae
    there is truth in that
    lit: when the river makes a sound, it's because it
        carries stones

(dar) la dura
    (to give) the hard truth
    lit: the hard

(dar) la firme
    (to give) the hard truth
    lit: to give the firm

caerse el casette
    to spill the beans (*idm.*)
    lit: for the cassette to fall out

abrir el tarro
> to spill the beans

irse de tarro
> to reveal secrets
> lit: to go away from the jar

sacar los trapos al sol
> to tell the secrets of others
> lit: to take the rags out into the sun

soltar la pepa
> to intimate something to someone
> lit: to loosen the seed

se le soltaron las trenzas
> he/she let it all hang out (*idm.*)
> lit: she let down her braids

meter la pata
> to give away confidential information or a
>   secret or to mess up in general
> lit: to put the foot

sepa moya
> no one knows

morir pollo
> to keep secrets
> lit: to die chicken

tejado de vidrio
> a life revealed to all, a life that's an open
>   book (*idm.*)
> lit: a roof of glass

Lies

hacer la pata
> to obtain something in a backward,
> underhanded way; to say nice things to
> someone to get something, flatter
> lit: to make the paw

dar la hora
> to kid someone, be ridiculous
> lit: to give the time

dar jugo
> to toy with someone, waste someone's time
> lit: to give juice

agarrar para el güeveo
> to play with someone

vender la pomada
> to tell tall tales, be like a used-car salesman (*idm.*)
> lit: to sell the ointment

hacerse el leso
> to play dumb
> lit: to become the injured

hacerse el ganso
> to play dumb
> lit: to become the goose

vendedor de pomadas
> liar, charlatan
> lit: an ointment salesman

ser más falso que billete de mil quinientos pesos
to be utterly false
lit: to be falser than a 1,500-peso bill

lágrimas de cocodrilo
false tears
lit: crocodile tears (like the English expression)

poner color
to exaggerate
lit: to put color

color (*n.m.*)
exaggeration
lit: a color

cahuín (*n.m.*)
lie

chiva (*n.f.*)
lie
lit: a female goat

chanta (*adj.*)
mendacious

de los dientes para afuera
they're just words
lit: from teeth towards the outside

de la boca para afuera
they're just words
lit: from the mouth towards outside

tomarle el pelo
> to pull someone's leg (*idm.*), play with
> someone (*idm.*)

tomarlo para la palanca
> to pull someone's leg (*idm.*), play with
> someone (*idm.*)

eso era el cuento del tío
> that was a lie (tall tale)
> lit: that was the uncle's story

Illicit and Violent Activity, Injury, and Death

One of the chief roots of Chilenismos is *coa*, a language used in the Chilean underworld. These words are often fleeting, because they serve as a code for robbers and other criminals who want to ensure that law enforcers do not nab them. However, the larger society of Chile has adopted many of these words, and they stuck in the daily parlance. They are often the most apt words for describing news of violence in Chile.

Criminal Behavior

tener malas juntas
> to have bad influences (e.g., scandalous friends)
> lit: to have bad associations

apretar cachete
> to escape, run away, flee

apretar cueva
> to flee
> lit: to squeeze the cave

perro muerto
> someone who "dines and dashes"; i.e., someone who takes something without paying and flees (e.g., from a taxi or a restaurant)
> lit: dead dog

chorear (*v.*)
to steal

cogotear (*v.*)
to assault

funar (*v.*)
to kill

gato de campo
a successful robber
lit: a country cat

mano larga
a robber
lit: long hand

güiña (*adj.*)
like a robber

lanza (*n.m.*)
a robber, thief

cana (*n.f.*)
jail
lit: gray hair

canero (*n.*)
a longtime prisoner

peni (*n.m.*)
penitentiary

estar precioso
to be in prison
lit: to be precious

pasta base
> type of cocaine

crack (*n.m.*)
> crack cocaine

palo blanco
> a guy working in league with illegal street
>> vendors
> lit: white stick

pato malo
> a delinquent, troublemaker
> lit: bad duck

paco (*n.m.*)
> a cop

Violence

dar un tatequieto a alguien
> to slap someone

picar la guía
> to incite, provoke
> lit: to sting the guide

avivar la cueca
> to stoke the flames

hacer la collera
> to try to fight

dar un zamarrón a alguien
> to shake someone

agarrarse a coscachos
to box one another

prestar ropa a alguien
to defend someone
lit: to lend clothes to someone

Cuidado, que el loco tiene fianza
Careful, he's got friends who can defend him.
(Careful, someone's got his back.)

aserruchar el piso a alguien
to injure, speak badly of

pica la jaiba
it's dangerous

sacar la mugre (a alguien)
to hit (someone)
lit: to take the dirt off

levantar las manos (a alguien)
to get ready to strike/hit (someone)
lit: to lift your hands

hacer pebre
to destroy something

ponerse los pantalones
to be a man (*idm.*), act tough
lit: to put on pants

sangre pato
in cold blood

gallo de pelea
> a good fighter
> lit: a rooster for fighting

cuero de chancho
> a tough guy
> lit: pig leather

Death

mala hierba nunca muere
> bad people never die
> lit: a bad root never dies

estirar la pata
> to die
> lit: to stretch the paw (foot)

parar la chala
> to die

irse al patio de los callados
> to die
> lit: to go to the patio of the hushed

estar doblando la curva
> to be nearing death, to be getting old
> lit: to be turning the curve

patio de los callados
> cemetery
> lit: the patio of the hushed

Miscellaneous Phrases

Schooling

jardín (*n.m.*)
nursery school

prekinder (*n.m.*)
prekindergarten, nursery school

kinder (*n.m.*)
kindergarten

colegio (*n.m.*)
elementary and junior high school

enseñanza básica
elementary and junior high school

enseñanza media
high school

liceo (*n.m.*)
public high school

enseñanza superior
college

pingüino (*n.m.*)
student in uniform

cátedra (*n.f.*)
test

control (*n.m.*)
quiz

lápiz mina/lápiz grafito
a pencil

ponerse al día
to catch up (in studies, etc.)
lit: to put yourself to the day

Competition

dar guaraca
to win easily, slaughter (*sl.*)

dar boleta
to win easily, slaughter (*sl.*)
lit: to give a ticket

de atrás pica el indio
we'll beat them (it's like a rally cry)
lit: from behind the Indian stings

baby fútbol
indoor soccer
lit: baby soccer

pepa (*n.f.*)
a goal
lit: a seed

Filth

caer las alas
    to have stinky armpits
    lit: for the armpits to fall

tener olor de rodilla
    to be stinky
    lit: to have the odor of a knee

una cantora/pelela/bacinica
    chamber pot

la media cantada
    dirty

dejar la (media) cagada
    to leave everything a mess

al lote
    very untidy, disorganized, messy

cochino (*adj.*)
    filthy

Adverbs and Very Short Phrases

al callo
    perfectly

de má'
    plenty, more than enough

nomás
    nothing more

de michael
certainly

de michael jackson
certainly

más encima
even worse, added to that

y todo el cuento
all that stuff
lit: and the whole account

y tanto
and such and such

nunca tanto
not quite so much

¿(Y) Qué sé yo?
Whatever; And stuff like that; And who knows
what else?

toda la cuestión
all that stuff

de todo
everything

algo por el estilo
something like that

a tu pinta
in your style/own way

te gastai
you have

Miscellaneous Phrases

más encima
moreover

a la chilena
Chilean-style

al agua
throw it out
lit: to the water

Hope and Optimism

las malas noticias vuelan
no news is good news
lit: bad news flies

peor es mascar laucha
better than nothing
lit: better than eating a mouse

le salió el tiro por la culata
it didn't turn out as I had hoped

más vale pájaro en mano que cien volando
it's of greater value to have the one sure thing
than to have many unsure options
lit: a bird in the hand is worth more than
100 flying

pan comido
something easily obtained or achieved
lit: eaten bread

menos mal
fortunately
lit: less bad

con suerte se llega al cielo
> with luck one gets what one desires
> lit: with luck one arrives in heaven

todo se paga
> there is justice in the end, it all works out in
> the end

Disappointment

le sale como las gueás
> it goes very badly (for him/her)

si no es pito es flauta
> if it's not one thing it's the other
> lit: if it's not the whistle, it's the flute

se mandó un condorito/una carga
> he screwed it up

me da lata
> it saddens me, it troubles me
> lit: it gives me (a) tin can

ser malo para
> to dislike, not enjoy
> lit: to be bad for

la mujer se le cortó la mayonesa
> it didn't work out for her
> lit: the woman cut the mayonnaise

Enjoyment

ser seco para
> to enjoy, like, do well
> lit: to be dry for

ser bueno para
  to enjoy, like
  lit: to be good for

me parece
  I like it, it seems good to me

Places

café con piernas
  coffee shop in which waitresses wear risqué
    attire
  lit: a coffee shop with legs

cuerpo bombero
  fire station
  lit: fireman body

bomba (*n.f.*)
  gas station
  lit: a pump; a bomb

ciudad gótica
  Santiago, Chile's capital
  lit: the Gothic City

gringolandia
  The United States of America
  lit: land of gringos

zona franca
  duty-free zone

Other Terms

Saben que a caballo regalado no se le miran los dientes.
Don't look a gift horse in the mouth.
lit: They know that when given a horse one doesn't look at its teeth.

En cuanto a gustos no hay nada escrito.
To each his own.
lit: In terms of tastes, there is nothing written.

pasar piola
to be quiet, to be overlooked

paja molida
boring, lame, rubbish
lit: ground straw

tener patas
to be full of personality, be bold
lit: to have paws

más chileno que los porotos
as Chilean as they get
lit: more Chilean than beans

huaso (*n.*)
country person (often *derog.*)

Yo soy igual aquí y en la quebrada del ají
I'm the same no matter where I am

chipe libre
full license to do what one wants, utter liberty

de tal palo tal astilla
> like father, like son

nada que ver/no tiene nada que ver
> completely distinct; it/that doesn't have
> anything to do with it

saber con qué chichita me estoy curando
> to know what you're getting into
> lit: to know what little cup of hard cider I'm
> getting drunk on

si querís también
> I'm not going to beg you, but I know you
> wanted it

güeá con pata
> something without a definite form, a senseless
> mix

me quiero sacar la espina
> I want to get the monkey off my back
> lit: I want to take out the thorn

no me ha tocado
> it hasn't yet happened to me
> lit: it hasn't touched me

The Profane and Sexual

This section is not for the meek of ear. However, it is an important part of understanding what is said in Chile. Often, conversations center around sex, specifically regarding who is with whom and doing what. Equally important are *garabatos* (expletives) that Chileans use freely and loosely. The creativity of the words and expressions on this list and the sheer number of terms goes to show that Chileans take profanity seriously, so go prepared. When there are numerous Chilenismo terms for one English term, I have put the English term first for reasons of clarity and brevity. In certain instances the English translations have been softened so as not to offend some readers.

Garabatos (Swear Words)

¡La cagué!
    I screwed up!

¡La cagó!
    He screwed up!

¡Chucha!
    Shit!

¡Por la chucha!
    Shit!

¡Cresta! ¡Puta! ¡Puta la güeá!
   Damn!

¡Por la cresta!
   Damn it!

¡Andate a la chucha!
   Go to hell! Get the hell out of here!

¡Conche tu madre!
   Screw you!

Sexual Acts

To have sex: comer a alguien, echar cachita, echar un pato, echar un polvo, echar una canita al aire, hacer las tareas, hacer un niño, tirar con tuti, ir a cachiyuyo, jugar luche, matar la gallina, papear, remojar el cochayuyo, verle el ojo a la papa, sacarle punta al lápiz, darle su merecido

una cacha
   sexual intercourse

botar el diente de leche, pisar el palito
   to lose one's virginity

no me ha tocado
   I haven't had sexual relations (recently)

comerle la color al vecino
   to have sex with the neighbor's wife/husband or
      girlfriend/boyfriend

hacerlo a la paraguaya
   to have sex standing up

irse cortado
  to have an orgasm

una cachiaspirina
  refers to how one will sweat heavily during sex
    and kill a cold

pegarse una buena cacha
  to have good sex

malo pa'l catre
  to perform sexual acts poorly, to be
    unimpassioned

prestar el poto
  to sell oneself, especially sexually

chusquear, putear, maraquear
  to sleep around

Grades of Sex

Grado 1 to kiss (each other)
Grado 2 to caress/feel up (each other)
Grado 3 to have sex (with each other)
Grado 4 to have oral sex
Grado 5 to have full sexual relations (includes 3, 4,
    and the rest)

Body Parts

butthole
  chico

rear end
  cototo, cuea

penis
> **banano, cabeza de bombero, cabeza de
> pájaro, cabeza de papa, cacho, callampa,
> canario, chacotero sentimental, chino
> tuerto, corneta, chula, cuatro letras, dedo
> sin uña, fiambre, guarifaifa, herramienta,
> huachalomo, instrumento, loly, longaniza,
> miembro, narigón con los ojos caídos,
> narigón pepe, pajarito, paquete, penca,
> pico, picoroco, picha, pichula, pirulín,
> pito, plátano, rollo de moneda, tula,
> verga, vienesa**

vagina
> **almeja, pelada/peluda, araña peluda, bistek
> con bigote, boca de mono, chauchera,
> chocha, choro, chorito, concha, corazón,
> cuchi-cuchi, flor, gatito, mono, osito de
> peluche, sapo, zorra**

testicles
> **bola, coco, huevo, hueás, pelota**

breasts
> **goma, melón, montaña, sandía**

Homosexuality

This book condemns homophobia in the strongest
of terms; however, it is not uncommon in Chile. In
order to help recognize all that is said, here is a
list of offensive expressions meaning that someone
is gay:

**se te quema el arroz, se te derrite el helado, se te
queda la patita atrás, se te apaga el cálifont, se te**

perdió la bandeja, te gustan las patitas de chancho, se le llueve la pieza

Pejorative names for homosexuals:

amanerado, cola, coliguacho, colizón, dulce, fleto, hueco, maricón, mariposa, nuco, redondo, sas

The adjective, *amariconado*, means effeminate or gay.

These derogatory expressions are used to either tell someone they are gay or lesbian:

el/ella es del otro equipo, se le da vuelta la camiseta, se le da vuelta el paragua, tortillera (lesbian)

Other Raunchy Terms

andar con cagadera
    to have diarrhea

churreteado
    full of diarrhea

hechar la corta
    to urinate

más lacio que la acelga; cacho paragua
    to be flaccid

levantar carpa; más tieso que saco de leña
    to be erect

me estoy arreglando la frutera
    I'm arranging my private parts

echar una canita al aire
    to do something behind your significant other's
        back (including committing adultery, as
        indicated above)

te hincho las hueás
    I'm screwing with you

sacar la chucha, sacar la cresta (a alguien)
    to beat up (someone)

mandar a la cresta/chucha
    to give a tongue-lashing

más que la cresta/chucha; más que la mierda
    a huge amount

viejo culíao
    asshole (person)

meca
    poop

hacer la pulenta
    to defecate

se me fue la carga pa' atrás
    that makes me want to poop

estar prendido
    to be gassy

echar la corta; hacer pichí
　　to piss

ese huevito quiere sal
　　that chick wants to get that guy badly

correr mano
　　to grope
calentar la sopa
　　to arouse your partner

se le chorrean las medias
　　refers to a a woman who is sexually excited

moquillo
　　sperm

se las saben por libro
　　they know all that's needed to know about sex

se le aconchan los meaos
　　one chickens out

chupapene, chupapico
　　an asskisser, brownnoser

**cambowarrier, putinga, choroloco, camboyana,
　　calzonera, chana, guerrera, warrier**
　　whore, slut

güehéta
　　jackass, someone stupid and easily manipulated

From Hippocrene's Chilean Library . . .

TASTING CHILE: A CELEBRATION OF AUTHENTIC CHILEAN FOODS AND WINES
Daniel Joelson

Tasting Chile contains more than 140 traditional recipes from this fascinating South American nation, spanning a variety of dishes that range from spicy salsas and hearty soups to the ubiquitous empanada and *manjar* (caramel cream) desserts. This book includes simple, everyday recipes, such as roast chicken and beef stew, as well as more exotic fare: blood sausage, fried frogs' legs, and rhubarb mousse.

Tasting Chile puts the native cuisine into context by describing staple ingredients and the influences other countries and cultures have had upon it. These exotic ingredients are described and substitutes are provided so that each recipe may be prepared in an American kitchen. Finally, the book includes a section on Chilean wines and wine recommendations appear throughout.

269 pages • 6 x 9 • 0-7818-1028-0 • $24.95hc • (23)

FOLK TALES FROM CHILE

This unique collection of fifteen folk tales represents a fusion of two cultures—the Old World culture of the Spanish settlers and the native culture of Chile's indigenous peoples. These classic stories will delight young and old readers alike.

121 pages • 5 x 8 • 0-7818-0712-3 • $12.50hc • (785)

Hippocrene's Spanish Language Guides . . .

SPANISH-ENGLISH/ENGLISH-SPANISH PRACTICAL DICTIONARY
35,000 entries • 338 pages • 5½ x 8½ •
0-7818-0179-6 • $9.95pb • (211)

SPANISH-ENGLISH/ENGLISH-SPANISH DICTIONARY & PHRASEBOOK (LATIN AMERICAN)
2,000 entries • 250 pages • 3¾ x 7½ •
0-7818-0773-5 • $11.95pb • (261)

EMERGENCY SPANISH PHRASEBOOK
80 pages • 7½ x 4⅛ •
0-7818-0977-0 • $5.95pb • (460)

HIPPOCRENE CHILDREN'S ILLUSTRATED SPANISH DICTIONARY ENGLISH-SPANISH/SPANISH-ENGLISH
• for ages 5 and up
• 500 entries with color pictures
• commonsense pronunciation for each Spanish word
• Spanish-English index
500 entries • 94 pages • 8 x 11 •
0-7818-0889-8 • $11.95pb • (181)

BEGINNER'S SPANISH
313 pages • 5½ x 8½ •
0-7818-0840-5 • $14.95pb • (225)

MASTERING ADVANCED SPANISH
326 pages • 5½ x 8½ •
0-7818-0081-1 • $14.95pb • (413)
2 cassettes: ca. 2 hours •
0-7818-0089-7 • $12.95 • (426)

SPANISH GRAMMAR
224 pages • 5½ x 8½ •
0-87052-893-9 • $12.95pb • (273)

SPANISH VERBS: SER AND ESTAR
220 pages • 5½ x 8½ •
0-7818-0024-2 • $8.95pb • (292)

**DICTIONARY OF LATIN AMERICAN SPANISH
PHRASES AND EXPRESSIONS**
1,900 entries • 178 pages • 5½ x 8½ •
0-7818-0865-0 • $14.95 • (286)

SPANISH PROVERBS, IDIOMS AND SLANG
350 pages • 6 x 9 •
0-7818-0675-5 • $14.95pb • (760)

Prices subject to change without prior notice. **To purchase
Hippocrene Books** contact your local bookstore, call
(718) 454-2366, or write to: HIPPOCRENE BOOKS,
171 Madison Avenue, New York, NY 10016. Please
enclose check or money order, adding $5.00 shipping
(UPS) for the first book, and $.50 for each additional book.